THE BEST OF
TECH TOPICS

Bob Livingston

TRAILER LIFE BOOKS

Production Coordinator: Robert S. Tinnon
Copy Editor: Judi Lazurus
Cover and Interior Illustrations: Randy Miyake
Cover, Interior Design, and Typesetting: Robert S. Tinnon

This book was set in Minion and Quay and
Printed and bound in the United States of America.

9   8   7   6   5   4   3   2

ISBN:0-934798-55-9

Contents

Electrical Systems   25

Drivetrain and Towing   37

___

Introduction

When we first kicked around the idea of running a column to answer readers' technical questions in *Highways*, Good Sam's official publication, we were a little apprehensive. Once we committed to such a column, we would have to make good on our promises. Would we get enough letters? Would we receive too many letters for our staff to handle? What about the diversity of the questions? And, could we answer them with authority?

I'm happy to report that the "Tech Topics" column is a resounding success: It's the most popular column in *Highways*.

As you might expect, we process a bundle of mail each month. Some of the questions are fairly easy to answer; some require a great amount of research. In any case, the questions we receive from our readers are well thought out; some are downright challenging. Two things we know for sure: RVs are complicated vehicles, and the RVer's quest for knowledge is awesome. In order to keep the column fresh each month, we rely on questions covering different topics. While editors of other publications may worry about finding new material each month, we rarely have to repeat subject matter. If you're a regular reader of "Tech Topics," you know that the questions range from simple appliance problems to mysterious maladies designed to stump even the most experienced technician. But we always find an answer! Some may disagree, but that's the beauty of the whole thing—the monthly dialogue is fantastic.

This two-way communication process not only provides answers that lead to solutions to nagging problems, but it allows us to learn, too. Everyone wins in the process.

As you might suspect, we have amassed a large number of questions and answers over the years. Readers continue to inquire about information published in past issues, and we constantly refer to previous columns when answering personal letters and e-mail. So it was logical to select the most interesting—and some of the most difficult—letters and answers published in "Tech Topics" over the years and offer the material in a bound book. Enter *The Best of Tech Topics*.

The book is divided into four sections: Major Appliances, Electrical Systems, Drivetrain and Towing Systems, and Interior and Exterior. Obviously, these are fairly broad categories, considering the complexity of the modern RV. If you are looking for a solution to a refrigerator problem, for example, check the Major Appliance section. Batteries and inverters make up a large portion of the Electrical Systems' pages. Drivetrain and Towing Systems covers the motorhome chassis, tow vehicles, and dinghy towing. The Interior and Exterior section is more of a technical potpourri; here you'll find discussions of rubber roofs, paint and stickers, holding tanks, and even safety devices, just to name a few items.

While the clearly delineated table of contents make perusing this book a snap, the real key is the detailed index in the back. Here, individual problems can be pinpointed very quickly. Although not all the topics will apply to your immediate needs, think about reading this book from cover to cover. We think you'll be amazed how much valuable information you'll retain. Then, when something comes up in the future, you'll be armed with the answers. And, with such knowledge, you're sitting in the captain's chair when it comes to dealing with repair centers.

Most authors take this opportunity to thank a few people who helped with the book. I would like to thank all the enthusiasts in the RV universe. Your letters are truly appreciated, so keep them coming.

Right now, sit back and enjoy *The Best of Tech Topics*. Hopefully, our paths will cross someday. Until then, I'll be checking my mailbox and e-mail.

BOB LIVINGSTON

Major Appliances

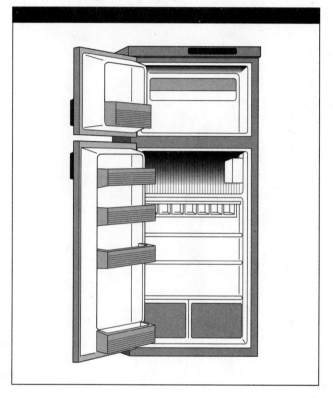

Bad Freon

I have been a travel-trailer owner for one year since my wife and
I purchased a late-1970s Shasta 25-footer. It came with a Coleman
air conditioner (a Mach III, I believe), added one year after the
trailer was new, which seemed to work fine. It worked okay for us
until we pulled it through the Blue Ridge Mountains to a campsite,
then it stopped cooling as if it had lost its Freon completely.

Once back home, we recharged it (not knowing any better) with
R-12 automotive Freon; again it worked great. In fact it worked
great for two whole months, blowing snowflakes until we pulled it
through the mountains. Five days after it had been cooling superbly,
it lost its Freon again.

We want to have the unit serviced, but are concerned that we
are faced with a leak problem that is undetectable until either an
incline or altitude is added to the equation. Have you ever encountered air-conditioning units that only leak in transit, up hills, or
at high altitude?

MARK JONES
LYNCHBURG, VA

Mark, I don't think the altitude or road grades had anything to do with
the air conditioner's failure. It's the Freon. Automotive R-12 Freon is
a low-pressure refrigerant that can slug up the system and cause it to
shut down. The problem is most likely not leak related; it just quit
working. It's truly amazing that it worked as long as it did. You should
have used R-22 Freon, which is a high-pressure refrigerant. Hopefully,
the system can be evacuated and pumped down so that the addition
of R-22 Freon will allow it to run properly. If not, you're faced with
buying a new air conditioner.

Backward Roof Air

We bought a used motorhome without an air conditioner on
the roof, so we had one installed. I was surprised to find the cooling
coils facing the front of the vehicle when I picked it up. The
mechanic said that as long as I had no generator for the AC power
to run the unit, it did not make any difference.

My concern is that the cooling coils will collect bugs, dirt, and other debris as we travel. Is the air conditioner mounted backward or is it okay?

FRANK R. ROSS
BODFISH, CA

Yes, the air conditioner is technically installed backward, but as long as you cannot use it while on the road, you're okay. Obviously, the air conditioner does not care which direction it is pointing while in use at camp—you can move your rig in any desirable position. But the coils have the potential of collecting bugs and other road debris that will restrict flow eventually. You could, though, cover the air conditioner while on the road, but that takes time and effort. The louvers, which are very soft, could also be bent by crashing birds, big bugs, and debris.

If you were to use the air in this position, the moving air while on the road would overfreeze the coils and lower the cooling performance of the air conditioner.

Generator Kicks Off

I have a 1995 Coachmen van camper with a 2.8-kw generator and an 11,000-Btu air conditioner. Since buying it in June 1995, I have had the problem of the generator being "sniffed out" when the air-conditioner compressor kicks in after it has been cycled off the first time. Sometimes the air will cycle off/on for an hour or so, and sometimes for a cycle or two before the generator stalls.

The generator has been load tested at two different Onan centers and is within specs. The rooftop air-conditioning unit has been replaced by Dometic. The temperature range during this time has been 80°F to 90°F, day or night, parked or running on the highway.

At home, using a stopwatch and a Fluke RMS amp probe, I recorded these readings: compressor cycles every two minutes or less; compressor running at 12 to 13 amps; when the compressor initially kicks in, the surge is recorded at 36 amps before falling to 12 to 13 amps. Sometimes the generator picks up the surge and sometimes it stalls.

Plugged into shore power, the amp readings and cycle times are the same in either case and a circuit breaker has never tripped.

FRED E. LULA
CONWAY, AK

Onan's 2.8-kw Microlite AC generator normally does a pretty good job starting and running an 11,000-Btu air conditioner. Because you ruled out the AC generator and air conditioner, it leaves little more to go on. Give Onan a call at (800) 888-ONAN and ask them to recommend a service center to have the unit tested a third time; output may be a little low and, considering that the air conditioner presents a sizable load on the AC generator, an adjustment may make a lot of difference.

In order for your particular AC generator to start the compressor cycle, the air conditioner must be equipped with an easy-start motor circuit that uses a relay/capacitor to help start the compressor. After the first start-up, the compressor maintains more pressure while in the rest period and the easy-start function helps the AC generator handle the load.

The Dometic air conditioner has this starting feature, but you might want to have it checked by a certified technician to make sure it's working properly. Because you're on the second air conditioner, I suspect the problem is elsewhere.

It's also possible that you are running other appliances while the air conditioner is cycling. Try a simple experiment: Turn off all the 120-volt-AC breakers except for the main and the one that controls the air conditioner. If the problem goes away, then concurrent loads are pulling some of the AC generator's amperage, leaving marginal power to cycle the air-conditioner compressor.

Switching to Generator

I have an Onan Genset III generator. Motorhomes I've previously owned were equipped with a plug that needed to be inserted into a receptacle to get power from the generator. With this one I just start and the power appears. What happens if ground power goes off and I start the generator? Do I have to unplug from service or just leave it alone?

RAY WOOLEVER
ELDRIDGE, CA

Ray, your motorhome is equipped with an automatic switching device, called a transfer switch, that defaults to the campground hookup if power is available. If it does not sense voltage from a 120-volt-AC source, it will allow the power to be provided from the auxiliary generator, providing it is running. You cannot damage any of the electrical circuits by allowing the auxiliary generator to operate while the rig is plugged into the campground power. Of course, you'll want to shut down the auxiliary generator immediately to conserve fuel and to avoid unnecessary running hours.

Oh, those Furnaces

I have a 1993 Award 723 with an 8520II Hydro Flame furnace. It heats to the set temperature and turns off the flame, but the fan runs for about 1½ minutes for the cooldown. After it cools to the set temperature, the thermostat closes, the fan starts, the fire lights, and almost instantly the thermostat opens. The fire goes out, the fan runs a minute or so, and it repeats the process. I have had the limit switch replaced, the DSI board replaced, and I am on my third thermostat. Can you help?

JACK PHILIP
PAHRUMP, NV

The problem you describe is called "limiting" by Atwood, the manufacturer of the furnace, and sometimes "short cycling" by RV mechanics. The first thing you should check is the voltage to the furnace. As we've discussed in this column in the past, the furnace requires a minimum of 10.5-volts DC to operate the gas valve. The fan motor would rather have closer to 12-volts DC. If the voltage is too low, it's possible the fan motor is running too slowly and, thus, opening the sail switch prematurely. Make sure the wires powering the furnace are at least 16 gauge, have good connectors, and are free of any corrosion.

It seems unlikely that the thermostat is the problem, since you have replaced it three times. Make sure the anticipator adjustment is correct. The directions for this are listed in the instructions. If the thermostat is made by Coleman, it needs to be grounded.

The last thing you should check is the condition of the ducting. Make sure the ducting is free flowing and not kinked in places. And it's important that at least three of the furnace knock-outs (providing holes for the heated air flow) are connected to ducting. Using two of the three, for example, can cause the limit switch to tell the furnace to quit heating.

Bad Furnace

I have a 1988 Collins fifth-wheel with a Dometic Duo-Therm furnace (model 20125.001). When we turn up the thermostat, the furnace will usually work properly the first time it ignites. But the next time it comes on, it—for lack of a better term—backfires, blowing smoke and fire 2 or 3 feet out the exhaust, and filling the RV with fumes. If we don't immediately turn the thermostat off, the backfiring will continue every few seconds.

The furnace has twice been removed and serviced to no avail. The air adjustment has been moved several times. A new regulator was put on the tanks. Whether or not we are hooked up to shore power makes no difference. The only thing we seem to have accomplished is to prevent the backfiring from occurring on the first ignition, which it once did.

CHUCK HALSTEAD
ALBANY, OR

Chuck, I assume you have quit using this furnace. The first thing you should do is take the furnace out and clean it well, removing any dust, dirt, or dust balls on the blower wheel. Pull the ignition-plug assembly and look for insulation that has broken off or become cracked. The popping and banging inside the combustion chamber create pressure that could blow a hole in one of the gaskets.

Leaking air into the burner from any source can cause backfiring. Look for holes around the collars in the heat chamber. If you have any holes in the heat chamber, it's time to buy a new furnace. Don't mess around with this furnace; it could cause serious injury if not fixed properly.

A good source for Duo-Therm furnace parts is All Seasons RV Appliance, Parts and Service Inc, 1150 Mitchell-Jellison Drive, Elkhart, IN 46516; (800) 344-0673. The company specializes in hard-to-find parts for RV appliances.

Heat Pumps

I have a new trailer equipped with one of those new Duo-Therm roof air conditioners with the heat-pump feature. The air conditioner is made by Dometic. We thought this unit had the newest in air conditioner technology, so we insisted that our dealer order it with the heat pump.

After reading the instructions, we're confused. The manual says that the heat pump will only work if the outside temperature is above 40°F.

We thought we could use the heat pump for supplemental heat when the temperature gets colder, not warmer. What gives?

JOHN EDISON
TAMPA, FL

The heat pump is designed to work in geographically mild areas and, you're right, will not function properly when the outside temperature dips below 40°F. During the heating mode, heat is removed from the outside air and released into the inside of the RV. When the temperature is below 40°F, there's not enough heat in the air that can be removed.

A heat pump works in two modes, heating and cooling. Refrigerant is reversed depending on the cycle. The system utilizes a compressor, evaporator and condenser coils, reversing valve, capillary tubes, an air-movement system (fan) and, of course, refrigerant. The evaporator and condenser act as either the inside or outside coils, depending on the operation cycle. When heat is called for, the compressor sends a high-pressure vapor into the reversing valve that routes the vapor to the inside coil, which in the heating mode is the condenser coil.

High-pressure vapor enters the condenser where it is cooled and condensed to liquid as it passes through the coil. Heat removed from the refrigerant is expelled to the inside air via the fan. Refrigerant leaves the condenser as high-pressure liquid. When the high-pressure liquid leaves the condenser, it passes through small capillary tubes, acting as the metering device in the sealed system.

A controlled amount of high-pressure liquid refrigerant enters the evaporator from the capillary tube. When this liquid reaches the low-pressure atmosphere of the evaporator, it turns into vapor. During this process, heat is removed from the air flowing through the evaporator, and the cool air is returned to the ambient air via the blower assembly.

Low-pressure vapor from the evaporator returns to the reversing valve that routes the low-pressure vapor to the compressor through a suction line, starting the heating process again.

Condensation Woes

In the fall, while using the furnace when the temperature outside is generally below 50°F, a lot of moisture condenses on the inside of our camper windows. Every morning I have to wipe the windows. Is there a solution to this problem?

DEAN E. KNAVEL
LEXINGTON, KY

Condensation is normal, especially if the furnace is working overtime. Also, metal window frames tend to sweat more than their wood counterparts, which are usually not used in RVs. The only solution, outside of continual wiping, is to use a dehumidifier. If you boondock camp, you can use the Dri-Z-Air portable dehumidifier. It's just a small basket filled with a special dry chemical that absorbs moisture. It's made by Rainier Precision Inc., 1150 Eastlake Ave. E., Seattle, WA 98109.

If you camp with hookups, you can purchase an electric (120-volt AC) dehumidifier for around $140.00. Sears is a good source, although dehumidifiers are available in most hardware and appliance stores. Don't be shocked if you pull out a number of pints of water at first, depending on the conditions.

Loves the Cold

In August 1995 I purchased my first travel trailer—a 1996 Terry Expo model 23 LV. I would like to use my trailer in winter to go on skiing vacations. I have inquired about this and have received responses such as, "You can only use your trailer in above-freezing temperatures." This is very disappointing being that I had planned to use my trailer throughout the winter. I need advice on how I can use my trailer in subfreezing temperatures (−15°F). I have a generator and can stand alone as long as the 35-gallon freshwater tank permits.

If you could send me tips on how I can safely use my trailer in subfreezing temperatures, I would appreciate it. The use of the bathroom and shower is essential.

ARTHUR CAREY
HEWLETT, NY

I admire your spunk, Arthur. I, too, am a winter-trailer user, but I am afraid we are in the minority, especially when it comes to camping in −15°F temperature. Most winter travelers use motorhomes in cold areas because they are usually better equipped to handle freezing or subfreezing temperatures.

The two most important factors are heat and insulation. Let's start with heat. Obviously, a fairly capable furnace is critical. If you have a 25,000-Btu or larger furnace, you're in good shape. I use a catalytic heater to supplement the furnace because it provides continuous heat without depleting the batteries, is easier on the propane, and makes a heck of lot less noise. When you get into seriously cold temperatures, your furnace is likely to cycle frequently. Keep in mind that catalytic heaters require proper ventilation and must be installed to manufacturer's specifications regarding clearances.

Make sure the heat is distributed evenly throughout the trailer. This can be achieved by adjusting the registers. Keep the cabinet doors cracked open so additional heat can get into the areas where the water and drain lines are routed. Try to limit entry and exit during the day.

As far as insulation goes, the best addition to your trailer is storm windows; there is usually a huge heat loss through the windows, especially if you have large glass areas. If this is not possible, you can make temporary window covers using ¾-inch R-Max insulation or other similar material. R-Max is foam insulation covered on both sides with a specially designed aluminum-and-kraft paper.

After cutting the insulation boards to size, I reinforce the edges with heavy-duty aluminum tape. If you cut these boards slightly oversize, they will press-fit into the window frames. Use a double layer for the roof vents. R-Max is available in most building-supply stores and a 4 × 8-foot, ¾-inch-thick sheet should run around $11.00. If you are using a catalytic heater, make sure you allow for proper ventilation when installing these insulating boards.

Drain and/or water lines that are routed close to the outside or are behind uninsulated exterior doors should be protected by either foam or fiberglass insulation. If your water pump is exposed, insulate it with fiberglass. Dump valves and sewer pipes are usually hard to protect without the use of heat tape, but you can increase freeze resistance by wrapping these fixtures with fiberglass insulation strips and duct tape. Heat tapes, which will really help, require 120-volt-AC power, so you'll have to run the AC generator if you want to go that route.

I always keep a gallon of water handy during the night in case all my preparations fail to keep the water lines from freezing due to unusually frigid weather. This water can be used to flush the toilet manually, if necessary.

Most of my winter camping is without hookups, so I rely heavily on batteries. If you do the same, two 6-volt, deep-cycle, golf-cart batteries wired in series are preferred over the one deep-cycle, 12-volt battery that usually comes with the trailer. I recharge the batteries by running the tow-vehicle engine at a high-idle speed for a couple of hours. Use 8-gauge wire for the charge line. If you have access to power, you can run the appliances for an unlimited time, but keep an eye on propane capacity.

Enjoy your winter travels . . . and keep warm.

A Bee's Home

I have a small problem and feel that if anyone knows, Good Sam will have the answer. When I arrived in Texas, I parked my Pace Arrow and noticed that bees began using the heater exhausts as home. I then purchased metal covers from a Pace Arrow dealer to place over the heater exhausts.

Recently I traded the Pace Arrow and bought a fifth-wheel. The first thing on my mind was to cover the heater exhaust. This time I went to Camping World and was surprised to learn it no longer sells the covers and they have a directive that they must pass on to the customers that states the warranty will be void if a screen is installed over the heater exhaust. I have not bought the covers, but everywhere I go that equipment is sold, I notice that the covers are still on the display.

Can you confirm the directive? If it is true, do you have another fix to keep the bees out?

LEWIS FULKERSON
ARLINGTON, TX

The reason Camping World recommends against using these screens is directly related to furnace-manufacturers' policies regarding covers for exhaust vents. Atwood Mobile Products, the maker of Hydro Flame furnaces, and Suburban Manufacturing Co., the other major supplier to the RV industry, do not approve of the screens. Apparently these screens keep the bees out, but they also can become clogged and restrict air flow. If air flow is restricted, the furnace can become a serious health risk, especially in a low-voltage condition.

RVers have been known to use duct tape to seal the exhaust openings, but this is also very dangerous. If you forget to remove the tape—and most of us have forgotten things in the past—the furnace cannot operate safely. Your best bet is to keep an eye on the exhaust vents and clean frequently if you know you have a problem with bees.

Old Furnace

I have a Sol-Aire furnace with a defective spark-ignition unit in my 1976 GMC motorhome. The spark-ignition unit is completely self enclosed, stamped Tri-Men Mfg., and has two male electrical springs.

I would greatly appreciate any assistance in locating a replacement spark-ignition unit. A temporary fix was to install a spark-ignition unit from a refrigerator. Upon ignition it pops rather loudly and scares everyone. I would rather have the correct part.

GERALD V. OLIVAS
SANTA PAULA, CA

Gerald, I don't think you'll like the news about your furnace because Sol-Aire went bankrupt in 1977. Your temporary fix is not very safe and, as a matter of fact, the only safe Sol-Aire furnace is a dead Sol-Aire furnace.

Rather than spend any more time and money on a product that has no available parts source, you should replace it with a new furnace from Suburban or Hydro Flame. It may take some modification, but a new furnace will work properly and, most importantly, be safe.

The only source of GMC motorhome parts is Cinnabar Engineering, Inc. 10836 W. Loyola Drive, Los Altos Hills, CA 94024; (415) 948-2618. Cinnabar Engineering is the licensee of General Motors for the manufacturing and distribution of GMC motorhome parts.

Weird Water Heater

I have a 1987 Airstream equipped with an Atwood model G6A-4E direct-ignition water heater. Several years ago, I discovered it would shut down in extremely windy conditions unless I opened the access door to the hot-water tank while the water heater was being used. Now the water heater will shut down under any weather conditions unless the door is left open.

It ignites and works perfectly with the door open. With the door closed, it can be turned on by the inside switch, will ignite and burn for two or three minutes, and then cut off.

BASIL HOLCOMBE
WALESKA, GA

It seems your water heater is starved for air. First, make sure the air shutter is adjusted correctly. Loosen the set screw, and open or close the shutter until the flame is predominantly blue with a short tip of yellow. If the propane/air mixture is too rich, the flame will be more yellow; if the flame roars, the mixture is too lean. Most likely, the appropriate shutter adjustment will leave approximately a ¼-inch opening.

Once you adjust the air shutter, remove the access door from its hinges. Pry the bottom of the door so that it allows a ⅛-inch gap when reinstalled on the hinges. This will allow air to enter the burner area. The door is installed too tightly in a number of these water tanks. I'm surprised you put up with this situation so long.

Plugged Orifice

We recently took our motorhome into an RV service center to have the furnace fixed. After removing the furnace, the mechanic found water and rust in the gas line. The orifice was clogged to such an extent that it had to be replaced. What really puzzled the mechanic (and us too) were the rust and water in the gas line. The mechanic said he had never worked on a furnace as old as ours (a Coleman that came with the motorhome in 1977) and wondered if the side-mounted propane tank (also the original) has water and rust in it that had worked its way into the gas line to the furnace.

About seven years ago, we had the propane tank recertified. We don't know what the procedure entailed, but we're wondering if the technician dropped the tank and inspected it inside. If not, we may have a serious problem with the tank. We certainly don't want to replace it if we don't have to, but will if it's unsafe.

NORMA REBENAR
CAVE CREEK, AZ

Norma, it's pretty unlikely the problem is with the tank. Vapor is drawn off the top of the tank. American Society of Mechanical Engineers (ASME) tanks mounted to the motorhome chassis are typically 14 inches in diameter. So for the water to be drawn into the lines, it would have to jump 14 inches before getting into the drop tube. Since water weighs approximately 8 pounds per gallon, and propane a little more than 4 pounds per gallon, this scenario of getting any quantity of water into the lines is highly unlikely. Even if it could happen, you would have an awful time with the regulator, and the other appliances would also not work.

Condensation is most likely your problem. Over time, this can amount to quite a bit of moisture. You probably know that when you turn the gas on after the propane tank has been off for awhile, there is almost always air in the line. The best way to bleed this air is to purge it from the range burner (while continually trying to light it). You can have this problem even if you only turned the gas off overnight. Without gas pressure in the line, you can get air breathing in and out by changes in atmospheric pressure. If the RV is left in storage for long periods of time, the air breathing in and out of the pipeline due to the atmospheric pressure can ultimately begin to condense moisture. Since your rig has been around for a long time, I suspect the moisture buildup over the years has done a real number on your gas-tube and burner assembly.

As for that recertification, I'm not sure what the technician did to the tank as recertification is not required of ASME tanks unless modifications have been made. Only Department of Transportation (DOT) cylinders require recertification every 12 years.

Propane Pop-off

During a recent trip, I had a bad experience with a propane tank that left me confused. I bought a tank at a discount store, had it filled in Reno, Nevada, and mounted it on my rig. We were on our way to Quartzsite, Arizona, for the big RV gathering when we smelled propane while taking a lunch stop. Our first reaction was that it was overfilled as the propane was leaking from the pressure-relief valve. Thinking I needed to purge the tank, I took it to an open area and opened the main valve. Nothing came out. This worried me, so I took the tank to a local propane facility and left it there (no service personnel were available at the time).

While this tank looked like my other one, it had threads on the outside of the area where the POL fitting screws in. What went wrong?

MARVIN WHITE
PORTLAND, OR

Marvin, there was really nothing wrong with your propane cylinder, other than the fact that it was overfilled—hydraulically full and causing the pressure-relief valve to open. Under the circumstances, you did the right thing by leaving the cylinder at the propane dealer's lot. Better to be safe than sorry, especially since the cylinder is much cheaper than the potential damage should leaking propane ignite.

Your particular cylinder is fitted with a Quick Closing Coupling (QCC) valve, a safer type of service valve that's commonly used on barbeques. As a matter of fact, you'll be seeing more of these QCC cylinders in the future because the RV industry will be using them in the manufacturing stage. When you opened the valve to purge the cylinder, the propane did not flow—that's precisely what the QCC valve is supposed to do.

The QCC valve has three safety attributes: If you open the service valve without having a fitting and hose attached properly, there's no flow of gas. It also has a "fuse" that will shut the flow of gas should the valve get hot (while in use) in the case of a fire. And if the pigtail should break, the flow would be restricted automatically.

If you find yourself facing the same situation—and you cannot find professional help—take the cylinder to an open area where there are no flames or sources of ignition and open the outage valve with a screwdriver. Make sure you are at least 10 feet from any flame or source of ignition, although 25 feet would be good insurance. The amount of flow from the outage valve is designed so that any flame or source of ignition that's more than 10 feet away could not ignite the escaping gas. The gas is regulated via a small hole, the size of a No. 54 drill bit. Continue bleeding the cylinder until the white vapor turns clear. The cylinder is now properly filled.

The threads on the outside of the valve indicate that the cylinder is fitted with QCC hardware. This valve allows the use of a 1½-inch ACME fitting with right-hand threads that require only hand tightening. A POL pigtail can also be used; gas will not flow unless both types of fittings are installed properly.

Overfilling by LP-gas service personnel is a common problem. If you get the cylinder filled in a cold-climate area and travel to warmer country, the problem is compounded. To eliminate this serious problem, the industry has decided to adopt the use of automatic stop-fill devices for cylinders. You should see these cylinders showing up soon. The industry has had many years of experience with automatic stop-fill devices in ASME tanks (chassis-mounted on motorhomes) with extremely positive results. With all types of RVs equipped with automatic stop-fills, the overfill problem should eventually go away.

Regulator Replacement

Last year my heater was acting up—sometimes operating and sometimes not. One RV place speculated that a new furnace should be installed. Plus, my refrigerator would sometimes need some coaxing to light. I just could not believe either was broken.

My problem was self-diagnosed over a period of time. I suspected the propane regulator, so I disassembled it, and replaced it with one from a barbecue. All the flames were good. Everything worked like new. I had been suspecting a partially restricted gas line to the appliances, but the person at the propane place who sold me a new regulator ($12.00) told me that these lines rarely plug or become restricted.

So as Paul Harvey says, "Now you know the rest of the story."

MARION R. HAWKINS
SAN DIEGO, CA

Although you "fixed" the problem, the use of a barbecue regulator is a serious no-no. A barbecue uses a single-stage regulator, and under 1995 code rules it is the only appliance that can use such a regulator. All other appliances, whether for home or RV, must use two-stage regulators. The RV industry pioneered the use of two-stage regulators in 1977, along with excess-flow fittings.

Single-stage regulators will have problems as inlet pressure changes, depending on the ambient temperatures. Barbecues get along fine with single-stage regulators, since pressure adjustments are not critical. RV appliances only operate properly at 11 inches of water column. Owners looking to save a few bucks by buying a barbecue regulator are only buying a lot of appliance trouble.

Another factor is the possibility of getting liquid into the regulator because RVs move around a lot. Two-stage regulators can handle a little liquid without adversely affecting the appliance operation.

Marion, I'm hoping that the last part of your letter means that you replaced the barbecue regulator with a two-stage version supplied by the propane dealer.

Had your RV dealer been experienced in LP-gas repairs, he/she would have performed a manometer test to determine that the regulator was defective. This is the first step in diagnosing propane problems. Had the dealer taken the 30 minutes to do the test, you could have kept the barbecue regulator attached to the grill and cooked a few extra steaks.

Sneaky Propane

I have a problem with my LP-gas system that has me puzzled. Twice while camping in 40° weather, my furnace shut down during the night. I thought that my LP tank had run out. But when checked, it was at least half full.

What should I do to prevent this from happening again and how does cold, even zero degrees, affect the LP-gas system?

LARRY GARON
BERLIN, NH

Larry, you did not give me very much information to go on, but I'll give it a try anyway. I assume the furnace was the only appliance to quit. If all the LP-gas appliances went out at the same time, I would first check to make sure your propane-leak detector is functioning properly.

In many cases, the solenoid that is used to automatically cut the flow of propane can close and, obviously, all the appliances will go out. This is usually caused by low battery voltage. Also, the furnace will not operate if the battery voltage drops below 10.5 volts.

If the furnace was the only appliance to go out—and assuming it works properly and battery voltage is not the culprit—then there are a couple of theories we can throw out. But first, let's discuss vaporization.

In cold weather, the quantity of the vapor is reduced, providing less pressure for the appliances. For example, a 20-pound cylinder that's half full will only produce 32,400 Btus of vapor at pressures of 10 psi or more when the temperature falls to 20º—barely enough to keep the furnace and refrigerator running. In another example, a 65-pound ASME tank that's 40-percent full will only produce 77,000 Btus of vapor at the same temperature and pressure.

Since the cold weather zaps vaporization, it's important that the quality—or mix—of propane is good. If you bought propane in the South or in Mexico, for instance, the gas may have a higher percentage of other "stuff," specifically butane, mixed with the propane. The common mix is 95-percent propane and 5-percent butane.

In cold weather the 5 percent would tend to accumulate, and continued refillings over time would reduce the vaporization to a point where the gas will do very little good or nothing at all. A tank with 40-percent built-up butane can produce only 3 pounds of vapor pressure at 40 degrees. Propane, on the other hand, will provide 10 pounds of vapor down to −25º. If the temperature goes much lower than that, then it's time to find a warmer location.

Keeping these vaporization numbers in mind, it's important that you are using a two-stage regulator. A single-stage regulator will provide 11 inches of water column (wc)—the necessary pressure to operate RV appliances—when the inlet vapor is 100 pounds. Since vapor pressure drops to 50 pounds in 40° temperatures, the single-stage regulator will let you down. A two-stage regulator will provide 11 inches of wc as long as the inlet pressure to the first stage is 10 pounds.

Also, if you have a two-stage regulator, make sure it is adjusted properly. If it is adjusted on the low side, say 10 inches of wc, a reduction of inlet pressure can cause it to further reduce vapor pressure to a point where the furnace electronics will shut down the flame. If the electronics do not read the right-size flame, they will shut down the flow of propane—a good safety feature. Furnaces (and direct-spark-ignition water heaters) seem to be much more sensitive to pressure drop than other appliances.

And remember, the greater the volume of LP gas in the tank, the better the system will work. So a full tank is always better in cold weather. If you feel that your tank is contaminated with too much butane, use it up now (to a tank level of less than 10-percent full) and refill it with the good stuff before the next cold season.

Refrigerator Problem

We have a problem in our 1993 Fleetwood Jamboree, and we've had it ever since we bought the motorhome new. Our refrigerator has a ticking noise when it's on electricity. We have had it in the shop four times and no one can find the problem. Last year the ammonia leaked out and the company (Dometic) replaced the board. We thought the problem was solved, but it isn't—it's still ticking. Can you help?

JOE CUTLER
WATSONVILLE, CA

The ticking sound is most likely a product of dirty DC voltage used to operate the refrigerator-control system. This malady is probably due to a problem with the control-wire hookup. Make sure the control wire is hooked to the battery side of the converter. When in doubt, connect this wire directly to the battery, or to a terminal in a fuse panel that is connected directly to the battery. Make sure this wire is fused at the source; a 3-amp fuse should do the trick, as long as this wire is only for the control panel.

If there is a voltage variation to the control panel, the relay in the circuit board will chatter—the ticking sound you are hearing. The refrigerator is designed to handle a certain amount of dirty DC power without adversely affecting normal operation.

It's also possible that an erratic ground is causing the problem. If the aforementioned fix does not cure the ticking, check the ground wires in the back of the refrigerator. The system controls sense the negative side of the wiring and, if the ground wires are dirty or loose, again, a relay can be chattering. Pull the ground wires loose, clean them carefully and secure them to the original connection(s).

If you lost the ammonia from your refrigerator, the repair center replaced the cooling unit, not the circuit board.

One More Time

It's confusing when RV shops give conflicting suggestions. I would like you to check and give us an answer. Should I or shouldn't I turn the refrigerator off while not in use?

D.M. WATFORD
GILBERT, SC

This is one of the most common questions we get during the year, especially at seminars. Therefore, we surveyed Norcold and Dometic, the manufacturers of the majority of RV refrigerators, to get the information straight from the "horse's mouth." In both cases, the answer was, "It's personal preference."

Because there are no moving parts in an absorption system, leaving the refrigerator on while the RV is stored will not shorten its life; neither will leaving it off. Based on this survey, it makes no sense to leave it on unless, of course, you want to keep the beer cold between trips.

It is wise, though, to clean the refrigerator thoroughly and leave it cracked open during storage. I even leave a large, opened box of baking soda inside the refrigerator to help absorb odors.

Weird Refrigerator

We have a problem with our Dometic refrigerator, model RM2807. When we turn on the fluorescent lights, the refrigerator begins clicking and "searching" from gas to electricity, and makes an annoying sound. When we turn off the fluorescent lights and use only the regular lights, the searching stops.

It doesn't make any difference whether we are using shore power or gas; whenever we use the fluorescent lights, the clicking begins. It has been this way ever since we bought the trailer two years ago, but we just realized that the searching only occurs when we are using fluorescent lights.

JAMES M. FIORINA
SAN GABRIEL, CA

Radio frequencies from the ballasts in your fluorescent light fixtures are causing the circuit board in the refrigerator to go whacko. This is especially a problem with older refrigerators, but can happen to newer models also. Normally, the fluorescent fixture closest to the refrigerator is the offender. To find the culprit, turn on the refrigerator and one fluorescent fixture at a time. Then replace the ballast or the fixture itself when you determine which one is affecting the refrigerator.

On the Level

On page 49 of the February issue of *Highways,* reference is made to the fact that a refrigerator must be level for adequate RV operation.

On page 52, however, the use of an electrical extension cord (250 feet) was considered, implying that leveling the refrigerator was not necessary when operating on AC power. Is this true? I always thought the refrigerator had to be level when operating either on propane or AC electric.

I would appreciate it if you would clarify this for me.

DON ADLER
TUCSON, AZ

It seems the leveling controversy continues to crop up. In the old days (approximately pre-1986), RV absorption refrigerators required careful leveling for proper operation. A good rule of thumb was to level the RV until about 75 percent of the bubble in the small, round level (provided by the refrigerator manufacturer) was inside the inner circle. This, of course, was determined by reading the level while positioned in the freezer compartment.

Absorption refrigerators use no mechanical pumps nor compressors to circulate refrigerant within the system. Therefore, proper leveling is necessary so that the refrigerant flow is maintained in the gravity-feed system. If the refrigerator is out of level, the refrigerant within the cooling coils will collect and stagnate in areas, and the cooling process will stop.

Presuming yours is a Dometic, you can determine whether or not you have an older unit by the square boiler-box cover (accessible by opening the vented outside-compartment door). If one of these refrigerators is allowed to run for a length of time in an unlevel condition, the cooling unit can become permanently damaged.

In square boiler-box units, the exposed siphon-pump tube will become superheated if the refrigerator is operated out of level. This allows the rust-inhibiting agent to chemically break down and restrict or permanently block normal refrigerant flow through the pump. "Burping" the refrigerator will not dislodge this blockage. If this happens, the only service is to replace the cooling unit, and that's expensive.

The newer refrigerators have an improved siphon-pump-tube design that drastically reduces the above condition when they are operated out of level, or when excessive heat is generated at the boiler section. The siphon-pump tube in the newer units is enclosed and surrounded by a weak ammonia solution that protects the pump tube from abnormal overheating. These newer refrigerators need to be leveled, but only to a point where the occupants are comfortable in the rig with no noticeable sloping of the walls and floors.

If the later-model refrigerators are operated in a seriously off-level condition, the cooling process will slow down or, in worse-case scenarios, stop. But the cooling coils will not normally be damaged and cooling should resume when the unit is returned to a more level condition. The shape of the boiler-box cover in the newer models is round.

The leveling routine is applicable for both electric and gas operation.

Now, about that 250-foot extension cord: The article you are referring to was not a technical dissertation on leveling refrigerators; it was a humorous piece and not intended to be taken seriously. We've always cautioned against using extension cords that are not rated for the load of the appliance.

Old Refrigerator Parts

We have a Sanyo refrigerator in our RV. The bulb went out and we cannot find one anywhere. It is a 15-volt, 10-watt screw-in type. There is no other identification other than "Sun" on the base.

EDGAR T. RIVERS
LAKE ELSINORE, CA

You can find the bulb you're looking for at Cool Fun, 15825 E. Edna Place, Irwindale, CA 91706; (818) 960-5456.

Smelling Ammonia

I have a Norcold refrigerator in my motorhome. When I opened the door, there was a strong smell of ammonia. What is causing this? What can I do to correct this? Please advise.

EARL F. KING
OLIVE HILL, KY

The smell of ammonia usually means the cooling unit is leaking and, most likely, there's a hole in the tubing or in one of the welds. The fix is to replace the unit. If your refrigerator is an older model, you might want to contact your dealer and ask if the unit you have is part of Norcold's rebate program. If it is, Norcold will give you a rebate when you buy a new refrigerator.

The problem is not related to owner neglect. There's nothing that you could have done to cause the damage, short of inflicting a blow to the tubing, of course.

Magic Cooking

We have a Magic Chef in our Free Spirit fifth-wheel. On our first trip, I tried to cook a pan of pasta but I couldn't adjust the flame on the front burner when the water started to boil. Not only could I not adjust the flame, but I couldn't turn off the burner either. The only way to turn the burner off was to turn the gas off. Needless to say, I was quite concerned.

We called the manufacturer and they advised that it was because we had not followed instructions in our book, which said that we were not to use a pan more than 1-inch larger than the burner. But nowhere in our book did that statement appear. I called them again and they said we had the wrong book. They sent a new book and new valves because there was a chance we had ruined the old ones by getting them too hot. We now have the new valves installed and we've been cooking on a small electric hot plate so that I can use a pot that is larger than 8 inches.

Would it be feasible to put some type of riser on the burner that would hold the pot up from the burner, thereby letting the heat dissipate? We have had RV ranges before and I could cook on them with any kettles that I had. I am not happy with the range as is, but do not want to go to the expense of having a new one installed.

RICHARD WHITE
DAYTON, WA

Richard, your problem may be in the position of the burners as they relate to the cooktop. Make sure the burners are high enough so that the flames are well above the cooktop. If they are not high enough, some of the flame may be actually burning below the cooktop and overheating the valves.

If the valves become overheated, they can bind and become difficult to turn using the knob. If you force the knob, you may strip the valve stem, thinking the valve is off when it's actually not, releasing gas and allowing the flame to continue to burn. That may be why the flame is only extinguished when the main gas supply is turned off. When the valves cool, resistance is lowered and the knobs may turn freely, completely cutting off the flow of gas.

If you feel the valves are binding, pull the knobs off and carefully turn the stems with a pair of pliers. This will allow you to determine whether the stems are actually turning and controlling the gas flow.

As far as the pan size is concerned, there are recommendations in most of the owners manuals. The company recommends that smaller (lightweight) pans be used so that the heat can dissipate around the pan and not be trapped at the burner or below the cooktop. This is especially true for a range with a high-output burner. Big, heavy pots and pans should not be used.

Gone to the Dogs

When we were in Florida, we turned on the air conditioner, locked the dog in the RV, and went on a sightseeing trip. When we returned several hours later, the air conditioner was not operating due to a power failure at the RV park. The dog was unharmed, but not happy. We were thankful it wasn't hotter outside. How can we avoid this problem in the future?

HOWARD MINER
NEW HARTFORD, NY

Howard, this is a good question, especially since I'm a dog lover and travel with a yellow Lab. I make it a practice never to leave my dog alone in the rig with the windows closed and the air conditioner operating. You never know when the power could be cut, the compressor in the air conditioner might fail, or any number of other maladies could kick in that can affect air-conditioner operation.

One option is to install a SmartGen controller, which will automatically start the AC generator when the inside temperature reaches a certain (preset) point. This may seem like a good alternative, but your AC generator must be in good working order and have plenty of fuel available. Keep in mind that there's still a risk of mechanical failure and you're dealing with the lives of your pets. The SmartGen is made by Summit Products Corp., Box 1508, Minden, NV 89423; (702) 782-3035.

I believe the best alternative is to park in the shade, if possible, and leave the windows open. An exhaust vent, like the one made by Fan-Tastic Vent Corp. (available at most RV supply stores and Camping World) provides good circulation of the air. If you're like me and have spoiled your dog, you'll feel bad that he/she has to "endure" the heat while you're away from the rig.

Make sure you leave plenty of water. I would prefer my dog be somewhat uncomfortable for a while, rather than succumb to heat asphyxiation.

Electrical Systems

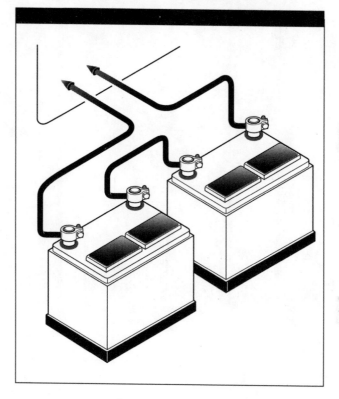

More Bouncy Bounce

I have a 1988 Chevrolet C-3500 dually with a 454 engine. I have a Tekonsha Commander brake control. While traveling last year with a cellular phone (bag phone) on the floor under the brake control, the phone was turned on (but not receiving or making a phone call) when a jerking motion started. This occurred a number of times within a short time frame. I remember reading in the wiring directions about making sure to route all wires as far as possible away from the radio antenna to prevent possible interference from the radio signal.

I shut the phone off and the jerking stopped. To prove this was the problem, I turned the phone back on and in a few minutes the jerking returned. One red light in the controller glowed very weakly.

JAMES A. BROWNELL
ROCHESTER, NH

I experienced a similar problem with my fifth-wheel, but the jerking was quite violent. It only occurred when I transmitted on my two-way radio. It took about two to three traveling days to make the connection between the jerking and my transmitter. Sure enough, when I traced the wiring installed by the radio shop, I located the loose ground on the radio and reconnected the wire using a larger screw and Holts No-Crode. End of problem.

I.D. BROWN
CLEARWATER, BC

You guys have stumbled on a good point that may indeed be a problem when running a cell phone or other type of radio communication. The installation manuals for the Tekonsha 9030 series and Commander brake controllers read, "DO NOT mount RF (radio frequency) items (portable phone, two-way radio, etc.) within a 1-foot radius of the control." While RF waves can cause erratic operation of the controller, the problem is fairly rare. The Sentinel model does not have this same problem.

Brake Controllers #1

We recently ordered a 1996 Dodge Ram 2500 Club Cab V-10 pickup truck to tow our 31-foot Airstream trailer. Standard equipment on Dodge Ram pickups includes power-assisted front disc/rear drum brakes with a rear-wheel antilock braking system (ABS).

Can we connect a hydraulic brake controller to this truck, perhaps utilizing the front brake port, or must an electronic type be used? We prefer the hydraulic controller for its smooth, even trailer braking.

JOHN AND SUSAN SWEARINGEN
ATLANTA, IL

The use of hydraulic controllers and the ability to tap into the vehicle's master cylinder became limited in 1988 when most auto manufacturers started offering ABS. The basic issue is the displacement of fluid necessary to make the hydraulic controllers work and how it would affect the operation of the ABS.

Due to liability concerns and the fact that the displacement issue is not unified among all the auto manufacturers, it's best to stick to electronic controllers on all ABS-equipped vehicles, especially the later models like yours. Kelsey-Hayes and Tekonsha, the two remaining players in the hydraulic-brake-controller business, recommend against using these units in ABS-equipped vehicles. Fortunately, advances in technology have made current controllers more practical and easier to adjust for smooth, efficient braking performance.

Brake Controllers #2

I'm getting our new 1994 Chevy Suburban, ¾-ton, four-wheel-drive diesel ready to tow. We're equipping the Suburban with new trailer electrical plugs and a new hitch. We bought a new Kelsey-Hayes hydraulic brake controller No. 81740C, supposedly the safest controller on the market.

Before undoing the fitting at the master cylinder, I thought I had better find out what to do if I get air into the antilock brake system (ABS). How do I bleed it? The manual indicates that special tools are needed, so I called our dealer who said, "Don't do it." Two other dealers had different remarks, but could not help. I called Chevy customer assistance and they recommended against installing the controller. Kelsey-Hayes said it would not affect the ABS unit; they claimed that the No. 81740C uses less than the .02 cubic inches of fluid the manual says is the limit.

The rear-wheel outlet on the master cylinder goes to a combination valve, which is the same unit used for many years, then to the Kelsey Hayes ABS unit. I am sure that by adding a T-joint at the master cylinder, the normal steel-brake-fluid line to the controller and then carefully bleeding, there will be no problem.

The electronic trailer brake controllers work, though they have several problems that do not spell safety. I want to have as much safety in towing as I can get.

Don Kellis
Woodburn, OR

There is a lot of controversy surrounding the use of hydraulic brake controllers in vehicles equipped with ABS. Chevrolet makes it very clear in its towing guide and owners manuals: "Don't tap into your vehicle's brake system if the trailer's brake system will use more than .02 cubic inches of fluid from your vehicle's master cylinder. If it does, neither braking system will work well. You could even lose your vehicle's brakes."

According to Kelsey Hayes, its hydraulic brake controllers fall well within GM's parameters. Therefore, it will be OK for you to install the brake controller on your 1994 Chevy Suburban. Ford and Dodge make recommendations, but they are somewhat vague. Most people reading the written statements of Ford and Dodge feel that both companies do not recommend installing hydraulic brake controllers on these vehicles. Kelsey Hayes recommends that owners follow the vehicle manufacturers' requirements.

Because of the potential liability, most dealers will not install hydraulic brake controllers on vehicles equipped with ABS. Some owners may even find it difficult to locate proper fittings because of the swing to electronic brake controllers. You should not find it necessary to bleed the vehicle's brake system, as long as you install the controller properly and follow the proper sequence. The only bleeding usually necessary is at the controller, and that's a very simple procedure.

Although hydraulic brake controllers seem to provide better trailer-braking sensitivity, electronic counterparts are certainly safe and, as a matter of fact, the newer models work much better than the older ones.

Batteries Using Water

I have a 1990 Alfa Sun 30-foot fifth-wheel with two marine/RV deep-cycle, Die Hard batteries. The manufacturer has checked the output of the converter, which seems to be OK. Therefore, can you tell me why I have to add water to the batteries about every 10 days?

RAYMOND RICHTER
FORT WORTH, TEXAS

Take another look at the converter, Ray. Most RV power converters limit DC output from 13.8 to 14 volts to prevent excessive gassing and loss of water from the electrolyte. Excessive gassing is also dangerous since hydrogen emitted from the batteries is very flammable. Check out the voltage at the batteries with a multimeter with the RV plugged into outside 120-volt-AC power.

If the batteries are sulfated, due to prolonged storage in a discharged state, charging will only cause bubbling (without conditioning the batteries) even if the voltage is correct. Check the individual cells with a good-quality, temperature-correcting hydrometer. The measurement of specific gravity (the condition of the electrolyte in the cell) will be 1.265 if the batteries are fully charged. By contrast, a battery that is 25 percent charged will have a 1.155 specific gravity measurement. Make sure you check the cells with no load on the battery 24 hours after the last charging. You can deplete the surface charge by running a 10-amp load for five minutes. If the batteries have been sufficiently charged and you cannot get a decent specific-gravity reading, chances are the batteries are gone.

Battery Wiring

I have a concern about inexperienced workers in auto-parts stores replacing batteries, which were originally 6-volt, wired in series, with 12-volt batteries using the same wiring. The damage to lights and appliances would be extensive.

You're a mechanic and would never do this, but it is a serious situation and many workers do not know the difference. Please let others know.

GEORGE ADAMS
BURLINGTON, N.J.

Good point, George. If your mechanic replaces 6-volt batteries with 12-volt counterparts, wired in a series, the voltage to the appliances and accessories will be too high. When 12-volt batteries are wired in series—one negative terminal to the other positive terminal leaving the other two terminals for hookup to the load—the power source becomes 24 volts, which can damage equipment.

Twelve-volt batteries must be wired in parallel: positive to positive and negative to negative. Make sure the connecting cables are heavy enough to adequately carry the load. Many service centers are unfamiliar with 6-volt, golf-cart batteries. If you are replacing your 6-volt batteries, make sure you inspect the job before you run the appliances and accessories.

Battery Fluid

While camping in the southland this winter, the subject of keeping water in the RV batteries came up. One fellow said white distilled vinegar was as good or better than distilled water. I wondered what you think about this idea?

JOHN F. KAIGHIN
LONGVIEW, WA

That's a new one on us, John. We've always used straight distilled water in all our batteries and I think most, if not all, battery manufacturers agree. Distilled water is free of minerals and other impurities that can cause problems inside batteries. I'd use the distilled water in the batteries and save the vinegar for the salads.

Deep-Cycle Batteries

What is the best way to connect two deep-cycle batteries in a motorhome? I have two batteries that are about the same age and have the same capacity connected in parallel to the circuit box. However, one battery seems to use more water than it should. Do I need a different setup?

JAMES RAY
TWIN FALLS, ID

James, I assume you have two 12-volt, deep-cycle batteries. If so, they can only be wired in parallel, which means the positive terminals are connected and the negative of one battery is hooked to the negative of the other, then the positive and negative leads are hooked to the fuse panel.

Parallel connection of 12-volt batteries usually reduces capacity over a long period of time. Also, it's critical that the batteries are the same brand, age, type and size when hooked up in parallel. In your case I suspect that one battery is somewhat different from the other and is causing premature deterioration.

If you want better capacity, try using two 6-volt, golf-cart batteries wired in series. When wired this way, you'll use the positive terminal from one battery and the negative terminal from the other battery for hooking to the fuse panel used to power the appliances and accessories, and connect the remaining negative and positive terminals with an appropriately sized cable.

Plug and Socket

We've been RVing for many years and love our travel trailer, but we've grown tired of wrestling with the connection necessary to allow the brakes and lights on the trailer to work while towing. We have the standard seven-way plug, which becomes more difficult to fit into the receptacle as time goes on.

It's amazing—we can put astronauts in space for days on end but we can't manufacture a simple plug and socket that works without busting our knuckles.

JOHN VINCENT
SEATTLE, WA

I could not have said it better myself. Most trailers are fitted with the flat-pin-style, seven-way plug and connector. Compatibility seems to be the problem. Although the molded plug and cord used on many new trailers is fairly well made, it often will not fit into the receptacle without a wrestling match. Blame it on poor tolerances or the fact that most of the receptacles are made in Taiwan. Whatever the reason, they don't seem to work well most of the time.

We ran across a receptacle that works like a champ: The OEM product Ford supplies with its trailer-towing packages. The quality is fantastic and it mates perfectly with the factory-molded plug and cord. It does not work as well with the two-piece plugs that can be hard wired, because these plugs are inferior in quality and function. The Ford receptacle has a nicely made spring-loaded door with a stop that actually holds the plug in place. And, if you don't know the wiring sequence, a wiring diagram is molded right into the face of the receptacle.

The receptacle was a part change for the 1994 models; last year's part was also of great quality, but not compatible with RVs. While the receptacle is the best we've seen, it does not come cheap, partly because you have to purchase the entire wiring assembly. The part number is F4TZ-13A576-A and it retails for $35.00. All you have to do is unwire the harness and retain the rubber boot for rewiring on your tow vehicle.

If your existing plug does not work well, you can retrofit a new molded version using a seven-way connector kit available from The Bargman Co. The part number is 51-67-525 and it retails for around $15.00 (available from RV-parts stores).

To install, you simply cut or unwire the existing plug, connect the color-coded wires with solderless terminals (supplied with the kit) and heat the shrink tube to the cable (also supplied with the kit). If you want a cleaner job, strip the wires, solder them together and use shrink tubing to finish the job. Remember, you have to slide the shrink tubes on first before connecting the wires.

The combination of the Bargman plug and Ford receptacle will make your trailer hookup much more pleasurable.

Inverters for Dishes

Can I find a 12-volt-DC satellite dish TV receiver or a compatible 12-volt-DC to 120-volt-AC inverter to use while camping without shore power? The low-power requirement (less than 100 watts) of the system makes it a natural for one of the many solid-state inverters on the market, but I have tried two different ones on my home unit and the resulting picture has not been watchable, probably due to the quality of the AC signal produced.

ROBERT P. ORDWAY
LOUDON, NH

To my knowledge, there are no satellite receivers that operate on 12-volt-DC power. Although you did not tell me which inverters you have used, I have a pretty good feeling what went wrong. Since most receivers draw around 22 to 34 watts, it's common to opt for a very small inverter, maybe one tht is only rated for 100 watts. If you do the math, it seems like you have plenty of power. But, these receivers, like most sensitive electronic units, operate on pure sine wave 120-volt-AC power. This is what you get from household electrical outlets. Cheap inverters normally produce 120-volt-AC current in square sine waves. That being the case, the picture will be distorted and probably much smaller than it should be.

Inverters with pure sine-wave output are available, but are more expensive and somewhat less efficient. Therefore most RVers use inverters with a modified sine-wave form that, in most cases, will operate virtually every appliance and accessory. The better the inverter, the closer the sine-wave form resembles the pure sine form of household current, resulting in better performance of the receiver. Although you do not need a high-output inverter to operate the receiver, you do need a higher-quality unit. Read the specifications carefully before you purchase the inverter. Also, try to avoid the ones that plug into your 12-volt-DC outlet (cigarette-lighter type) unless you know the wiring is fairly substantial. Many times manufacturers wire these receptacles with 18-gauge wire that can create problems for many inverters.

Inverter Sense

I installed a Kenmore 120-volt-AC bar/dorm-type refrigerator in our Jayco 1206 fold-down camper, replacing the factory unit. We soon discovered an added convenience with this set-up. When preparing for short stops close to home, we placed precooled food and frozen meats in the fridge that was plugged in and also precooled for several hours. Upon arriving at our destination, our food is cold and we simply plug into the campground electric service avoiding the hassle of transferring food from an ice chest to the refrigerator.

Would there be any harm to the compressor in running this type of refrigerator off a power inverter (Statpower PC 300) hooked up to the tow vehicle's battery while en route on longer trips of several hundred miles? This would also be handy for us to use if we were to stop for an extended period of time while pulling the camper and wanted to leave the food in the fridge.

TODD A. BLACKWELL
OSAGE BEACH, MO

Todd, you can use an inverter to power the small refrigerator, but the one you are looking at might not work. The PC 300 is designed primarily for resistive loads, such as lighting. It does not have a very good surge rating. The Pro-Watt 250 would be a better bet since it has a higher surge power rating. Keep in mind that most small compressor refrigerators are rated at 1.1 to 2 amps. The Pro-Watt 250 will only work if your refrigerator has the lowest rating. Surge power requirements are usually 2 to 5 times that of the continuous rating.

Although it's somewhat overkill for your situation, you might consider the Pro-Watt 800. It's always good to know you have plenty of power for keeping food at proper storage temperatures. Since you are probably restricted to one battery, you'll only be able to run the refrigerator while on the road. Make sure you have at least an 8-gauge charge line and that you remember to turn off the refrigerator when making stops or in camp without hookups. It's still a good idea to load the refrigerator with cold/frozen foods to give the cooling process a heat start.

Better Connections

We have a 1993 Dutchmen 22-foot fifth-wheel that we bought when it was a year old. Twice I have had to redo the brake-wire connections—the 25-cent blue connectors. Evidently they corrode slightly and lose their contact with the wire (sometimes only partially). We had a 1956 Shasta trailer for 27 years and the brakes never needed any attention. Is there a way to improve the connections?

DENNIS M. ERICKSON
AITKIN, MINN.

Unfortunately some manufacturers are addicted to quick connectors—wireless terminals that allow the attachment of a second wire by tapping into an existing wire. While they have a place in certain wiring jobs, they do not fare well when exposed to the elements. A better method is to use butt connectors with ends that can be heat-sealed to the wire. Once the connecting wires are stripped and crimped in place, the ends of the terminal are exposed to heat, melting the plastic and insulating material around the wire. Done right, the connection will be virtually watertight and impervious to corrosion.

If you cannot find these terminals, use a good-grade butt connector and shroud the entire splice with heat-shrink tubing. Remember to slide the heat-shrink tubing on before making the connection. This procedure also provides a tight seal.

A number of manufacturers use wire nuts, which are worse than quick connectors. Their reasoning: They can be removed, releasing the wires when the brakes need servicing. I'll take my chances with losing a half inch of wire by cutting off the sealed butt connectors when servicing is required.

Various Lightbulbs

I have a 1993 Shasta motorhome with No. 1141 lightbulbs in the taillights and have found that No. 1156 bulbs are cheaper and give off more light. Why the difference and will the No. 1156 damage my taillights?

JIM MINNIS
WILMOT, WI

Jim, the No. 1141 lightbulb has a 21-candlepower (CP) rating; the No. 156 has a 32-CP rating. Therefore, the No. 1156 is brighter and gives off more heat. The No. 1156 should be more expensive, even though you've found a source that is cheaper. In any case, most RV taillights are designed to use the No. 1141 bulb. If you use the No. 1156 bulb you're risking the chance of melting the lenses. Unless you can verify that the lenses you're using are rated for the brighter bulbs, I would go back to the No. 1141 bulbs.

Drivetrain and Towing

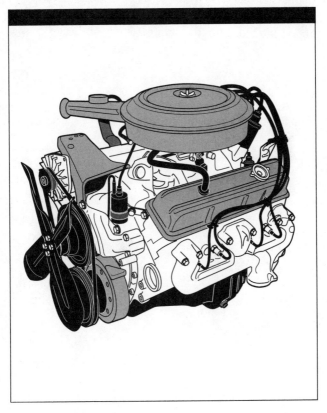

Using Dash Air

I would like to know if I should use my dash air conditioner to cool my motorhome when traveling? I was told by a few nonprofessionals that I should be using my roof air to cool my motorhome when on the road.

They claim the dash air overloads the motor and causes excess wear and tear. Being a driver and not a mechanic, I don't know the answer. My rebuttal at the time was why did they put it in if you're not supposed to use it?

KEN KIBLER
JENSEN BEACH, FL

There's no reason why you can't use the dash air conditioner, Ken. It will zap your power somewhat, but in most cases you can't feel the difference. You will, though, use a few more gallons of fuel during the trip. Your temperature gauge should tell you that you are not creating excessive heat by using the air conditioner.

Unless you have a very small motorhome, the dash air conditioning will not cool the interior sufficiently during hot weather. That's why most people run the auxiliary generator and roof air(s). The dash air conditioning becomes a supplement and can help, especially if you have large expanses of windshield glass and a very hot sun overhead.

Deflecting Wind Drag

We pull a 22-foot Dutchmen trailer with a 1991 Chevrolet truck that has a 6.2-liter diesel engine and a 3.73 rear-end gear ratio. The only problem that we encountered towing was when there was a very strong headwind, as is often the case in the western deserts. I'd like to know more about the effectiveness of wind deflectors.

I've noticed that many semi trucks have them and feel that these companies would not have spent a lot of money to purchase them if there wasn't some benefit. If it increases fuel mileage, wouldn't it also affect performance against such headwinds? If purchasing one, what features would be most important to consider?

TOM LEWANDOWSKI
ELM CITY, NC

Adding a wind deflector is not as simple as hanging a piece of sheet metal or fiberglass on the roof of your truck. Calculating the proper positioning and deflection angles is quite a science, incorporating many aerodynamic factors. Obviously, the truckers are sold on them. But consider that even a negligible fuel-economy improvement for long-haul truckers is worth the investment since the original cost can be amortized over countless miles. Most RVers roll up relatively few miles over the life of their rigs by comparison.

If you decide to add a wind deflector, contact a company that has experience with both semi trucks and RVs. These people understand aerodynamics and will be able to equip your truck with a deflector that has the proper size, shape and angle of deflection and the best advantages for improving wind drag. A good place to start is Wingmaster, 9272 Borden Ave., Sun Valley, CA 91352; (818) 504-2388. This company offers a line under the Aerotravel label.

Brake or Downshift?

I have a 22-foot motorhome, 11,800-pound gvwr, a 454 Chevrolet engine with an automatic transmission and 53,000 miles on the odometer. A recent lining check of brakes revealed very little wear. I've always downshifted for stops and on downgrades.

Am I saving brake lining at the greater expense of my transmission?

GEORGE F. ECKBLOOM
LA MESA, CALIF.

Downshifting to slow your coach, especially in a hurry, will certainly help with the overall braking and should not create any adverse wear problems with the transmission. Generally, if you can use your transmission to help with braking or climbing a grade, use it. If you don't mind manually shifting, continue the practice; the potential savings in maintaining your brakes will pay for the slight inconvenience.

A good rule of thumb is to allow the transmission to do its own thing while driving at 25-30 mph in slow traffic. When driving 45–50 mph, and the need to brake arises rapidly, drop the tranny into second gear and allow compression braking to help with the slowdown. In the Turbo 400 transmission, for instance, the over-run band during compression braking prevents the direct drum from turning in the opposite direction. That's the only use for this band and since it's not affected by torque or horsepower, the downshifting process will not harm the transmission.

Conversely, it also makes good sense to drop into second to maintain speed when climbing grades. I always downshift at 45 to 50 mph and prefer to do my shifting manually rather than use full throttle and "kick down" the transmission. Make sure you don't exceed 3500 rpm during downshifting.

Brakes and Bearings

I hope you can help me with a bearing and brake problem on my 1987 25-foot Okanagan fifth-wheel. The weight is approximately 7,000 pounds, it has four-wheel electric brakes and I tow it with a 1992 Dodge diesel pickup.

It has a Kelsey brake control and, if set up so the trailer brakes work properly, after three to five stops or slowdowns, the bearings and drums get too hot. In fact, I have had two bearing failures in the past year. If I slacken the control so there is no heat buildup, I don't have nearly enough stopping power.

The pendulum-control indicator is in the up-and-down position. In the past four years, in addition to the two failures, all the bearings, races, brake shoes and springs were replaced. I put about 10,000 miles on the rig each year. I can't help but think this is an electrical problem.

J. PETER ROBERTSON
PORT ALBERNI, BRITISH COLUMBIA

We own a 1992 26-foot Dutchmen travel trailer that weighs 5,500 pounds loaded; 1,000 pounds of this is tongue weight, leaving 4,500 pounds to be carried by the two axles. Each axle is rated for 3,500 pounds (7,000 pounds total), so you see we have plenty of reserve capacity.

The problem is that I have been burning out wheel bearings, replacing them on three occasions.
I believe the problem relates to the way the bearings are packed with grease and what type of grease is used.

JOHN L. FLITZ
LAKE ANN, MI

Brake drums that run excessively hot are usually caused by linings that are adjusted too tight. The star wheel should be adjusted until the wheel turns with a noticeable drag, then loosened slightly. Other factors may be a drum that is severely out of round or linings that have been installed incorrectly. Check the linings for uneven wear patterns; if they are tapered, installation may be suspect.

Another consideration is leaking current from the breakaway switch or brake controller. There should be no voltage (enough for activation) at the magnets unless the controller is activated or until the breakaway switch plunger is pulled. You can measure this with a multimeter. Inspect the magnets. If they have a yellow or blue discoloration, it's possible they are being overactivated, maybe even when braking is not called for.

Bearings play a critical role. I assume both of you have the correct bearings for the axle. I would check with the axle manufacturer just to verify part numbers. Bearings must be whistle clean, free of any burrs and other defects and packed with high-temperature grease. Make sure grease is forced between all the rollers.

Look for hot spots on the drum. If the drum is wearing evenly and showing hot spots, then the bearings may be too tight. If the drums are wearing to one side, suspect bearings that are not set properly. Make sure the races are not warped.

When installing the bearings, make sure they are first preloaded. To do so, tighten the castle nut until it is snug or at 50 foot-pounds (if you have a torque wrench available) while turning the drum counterclockwise. Stop spinning the drum and loosen the castle nut. Hand tighten the nut, line up the holes in the spindle and install a new cotter pin.

Exhaust Brakes #1

I am getting a Dodge Cummings diesel, ¾-ton truck. I would like to know if I need anything like the product called Mountain Tamer, or one called U.S. Gear D-Celerator Diesel Exhaust Brake, when going up and down mountain grades? The Dodge dealers say no; they say to just take it out of overdrive, and that is about all they know.

When going up mountain grades, do I need to shift the automatic to second gear, then into first? When going down, do I shift to first so I do not have to step on the brakes all the way down the hill? I am pulling a 25-foot fifth-wheel with a gvwr of 8,000 pounds.

I read that you could ruin the diesel engine when going down hills if you do not have one of these products installed. Can you help me?

PERCY KLEINSCHMIDT
GLENDALE, AZ

Diesel engines have limited engine braking; therefore, when you start pulling very heavy loads (or have a large motorhome); downhill speeds can become a concern. You should do all right towing your 25-footer, but an exhaust brake will surely add a great amount of control while descending grades. However, you definitely will not ruin your diesel if you don't install an exhaust brake.

There are four popular manufacturers of engine (exhaust) brakes designed for diesel engines:

Cummins Engine Co., Inc
(Rambrake/Extarder)
P.O. Box 3005
Columbus, IN 47202
(800) 343-7357

Decelomatic Corp.
4837 E. Indian School Road,
Phoenix, AZ 85018,
(602) 956-8200;

U.S. Gear Corp.,
9420 Stony Island Ave., Chicago, IL 60617,
(800) 874-3271;

Valley Fuel Injection (BD Engine Brake),
Box 231, Sumas, WA 98295,
(800) 887-5030.

You'll need to downshift and upshift according to conditions while towing your trailer. Downhill, you should not run in overdrive. If necessary, slow down and downshift to second gear. When driving uphill, you'll need to downshift on any grade that causes the truck to reduce speed. Remember that with the diesel you can only downshift as long as you remain in the engine's rpm range. High speed downshifting will only cause the engine to quit building power when it exceeds its safe rpm range. Your tachometer should be able to help you here.

Exhaust Brakes #2

I recently purchased a new motorhome built on an Oshkosh chassis with the Cummins 230-hp engine and the Allison MD3060 transmission. I wanted to install an exhaust brake, but an employee at a Cummins facility said they do not recommend using an exhaust brake with an automatic transmission.

I would like to know your opinion and experience with an exhaust brake used with this automatic. Does it offer a large enough braking force to be worth the cost? Is there any problem keeping the transmission locked in the lower gears? Would it be advisable to install the stronger exhaust springs if the exhaust brake is installed? Are there any special requirements to use an exhaust brake with the Allison MD3060?

MILTON SCOTT
PRINCETON, TX

Milton, it seems strange that someone at Cummins told you that the company does not recommend using a retarder since Cummins markets its own exhaust-brake system. It's called the Extarder and it is designed to be used on all Cummins B- and C-series engines.

According to Cummins, its Extarder is good for 190 hp of braking, which will do a good job of slowing down the load without excessive use of service brakes. If you want extra braking insurance for your heavy motorhome, an exhaust brake is a good investment. You will have to install heavy-duty exhaust valve springs before installing the Extarder.

There should not be any special requirements in using an exhaust brake. These systems use engine exhaust pressure to slow you down. Exhaust gases are restricted, thus increasing back pressure that creates resistance against the pistons, slowing down the crankshaft.

It's a simple concept that works well. Installation is also very easy in most applications. While, for obvious reasons, Cummins recommends the Extarder system, the company has not put the kabash on other brands of retarders on the market.

Better Brake Fluid

I have a 33-foot Airstream motorhome with a 454 Chevrolet P-30 chassis. I am presently using Dot 3 brake fluid but have heard that Dot 5 is far superior. Do you advise changing to Dot 5?

WILLIAM R. GROSSE JR
FOX LAKE, IL

Basically, Bill, it's best to follow the recommendations stated in your owner's manual. The difference between the two is the chemical base of the brake fluid. Dot 5 has a silicone base, which makes the fluid less susceptible to moisture retention. It also has a higher boiling point. Because of its chemical makeup, Dot 5 fluid resists corrosion and vaporizing better than Dot 3 or 4.

If moisture is present in the fluid, it can vaporize when the temperatures get very hot, causing a possible mushy brake pedal. Of course, corrosion in the lines limits the hydraulic action of the brakes.

Although Dot 5 seems to have better properties than conventional fluid, you cannot mix the two. Many later-model vehicles can use Dot 5; before you change over, the lines must be pressure purged (bled) of all Dot 3-4 fluid. It's even a good idea to change the wheel cylinders before using Dot 5 in older vehicles. Remember, consult the owner's manual first.

While we're on the subject, it's a good idea to pressure purge your brake system every couple of years, regardless of the type of fluid you're using. This is somewhat controversial among engineers and mechanics, but cleaning out the system and adding new fluid (an inexpensive procedure) seems to make good sense.

Needs GM Chassis Info

I own a 1987 Sprinter by Mallard on a Chevy chassis. When I tried to have the front end aligned, the service center said they would be glad to do it, but they have not been able to get the "P" specs to do the job. They have tried everywhere but have had no luck. Can you help with this problem?

EUGENE ATKINSON
BLOOMINGTON, IN

The information your dealer is looking for can be found in the *Chevrolet Motor Home Chassis Service Guide,* often referred to as "the orange book." This guide offers comprehensive information valuable to all P-chassis owners, and detailed alignment specifications are listed.

You can obtain a copy of this guide by calling (800) FOR-CHEV.

Coolant Additives

I understand that cooling/overheating protection is critical on the Ford 1995 diesel. I also understand that some additives that improve coolant performance must be added to protect the engine.

Can you clear up my confusion on this matter before I spend bucks on unneeded additives or a costly rebuild?

R.E. Buyer
Medford, OR

There is a coolant additive that's recommended for 1995 and newer Ford trucks. According to the owner's and service manuals, this additive is recommended every 15,000 miles. This stuff is designed to neutralize the acids in the coolant and act as a rust inhibitor. It comes in 10-ounce cans and the price will vary from dealer to dealer. We found it for as little as $8.17 a can and as much as $22 by calling various dealers. It's Motorcraft part No. FW-15.

Cooler Routing

In the May issue, you discussed transmission cooler installation. You specified that it is generally preferred to route oil from the transmission to the radiator and then to the auxiliary cooler.

In the May issue of one of your competitor's magazines, the author suggested going through the auxiliary cooler first and then the radiator.

Paul E. Conaway
Vista, CA

Paul, this question has many answers depending on who you talk to, but the consensus among the cooler manufacturers and mechanics who have RV-engine experience is to route the cooler after the radiator. This provides the coolest temperatures for the transmission oil.

One reason for running the cooler before the radiator is extremely cold weather. In frigid temperatures, the oil can become overcooled unless it is run through the radiator before returning to the transmission. If climate is a concern, it may make more sense to bypass the cooler in the winter and retain the optimum cooling efficiency during the summer.

Some technicians believe that running the cooler before the radiator helps with engine temperature if the vehicle is used to pull ultraheavy loads. But this thinking is pretty much going by the wayside since late-model radiators are so efficient that the hot transmission oil entering the radiator tank has little or no effect on temperature control of the coolant.

Here's a letter from George Cargo, national sales manager of Tekonsha Engineering Co., who offers another solution to the oil-cooler-line-routing controversy:

"Regarding the article about automatic-transmission oil-cooler installation in the May issue of *Highways,* let me apprise your readers of an auxiliary cooler designed to address questions posed in your column.

"Tekonsha Engineering recently introduced the Defender SR (Self Regulating) auxiliary-transmission oil-cooler design. It's thin-line (¼-inch thick), stacked-plate construction incorporates two bypass plates within the cooler core.

"As the transmission fluid under pressure enters the auxiliary cooler, the temperature and consistency of the fluid determines the oil-flow path. If the fluid is cool or sludgy, as in a cold start-up or cold-climate situation, the fluid will bypass the main cooling plates of the cooler through the self-regulating plates.

"As fluid temperature increases and the transmission oil thins, fluid cycles through all cooling plates within the Defender's core, providing necessary auxiliary cooling.

"This design feature provides the required, on-demand auxiliary cooling necessary for increased temperature periods while not overcooling the fluid. The self-regulating feature allows the cooler to dictate required cooling while minimizing pressure drops within the heat-exchange system, and without the need for installation of additional valves or mechanical regulators.

"The Defender SR is available in two gross vehicle weight (gvw) ranges: 11,000-18,000 pounds and 18,000-24,000 pounds. It is recommended for installation on the transmission return line from the radiator cooler to the transmission. The kit comes complete with all necessary hardware and auxiliary hose and is available through all RV dealers who carry Tekonsha's line of recreational vehicle products."

Engines and Oil

In December 1995, the 454 engine in my 1993 Winnebago Brave was replaced. The invoice referred to the engine as a "new Mark V." I've asked both the dealer and General Motors to explain the difference between my original engine and the replacement, but neither could give me an answer.

Also, my oil-pressure gauge fluctuates erratically. It will go from a normal of 60 psi at cruise rpm and 45 psi at idle to 45 psi at cruise rpm and 30 psi at idle. This change can occur while at cruise or at idle. Again, neither the dealer nor GM could explain why. The only answer I've received was "electronic gauges do that."

FLOYD M. HAYES
PALMDALE, CA

Floyd, the 7.4-liter Mark V is a later-generation engine that is designed to be more durable than the Mark IV. Since the Mark V engine was introduced in late 1993/early 1994, the chances are your original engine was a Mark IV. The earlier engines were fitted with an adapter plate on the intake manifold for accommodating the throttle-body-injection system (TBI). Basically the engine was the "old standby" with modifications for the TBI. Your replacement engine features a number of upgrades, including an intake manifold designed for the TBI. Other improvements include a one-piece rear crankshaft oil seal, one-piece pan seal and a new hydrodynamic front crank seal that helps prevent leaks.

The Mark V also has a more efficient electronic spark-control system with the sensor mounted in a better location. The thrust-bearing surface is larger, the oil galleries are better and the heads are improved. Added are cast-aluminum valve covers. In a nutshell, you're much better off with this later engine.

As for the oil-pressure fluctuation, the problem is a defective sending unit. Apparently the design of this sending unit was not robust enough and a number of owners have experienced the same problem. Replacing the sending unit should do the trick since the new ones are improved, according to GM.

Gas-Gauge Accuracy

I have a 1979 Honey 23-foot motorhome with a 360 Dodge engine. I had a replacement fuel tank installed in the summer of 1994. When I took it out of storage in the spring of 1995, the gas gauge, temperature gauge and dash lights quit.

My mechanic installed a new temperature gauge and fixed the dash lights, but the gas gauge will only register three-quarters full with a refill. He installed a new sending unit with no luck. What do you suggest?

CARL R. SIMPKINS
SOUTH BEND, IN.

I assume the mechanic replaced the fuel gauge with a factory replacement, in which case the diagnosis is easier. The sending unit may still be your problem. Most of the Dodge sending units have the float and pickup tube built into a single unit. The proper sending unit will register 8 to 12 ohms when the float is at the top position (when the tank is full); the resistance is 73 ohms when the tank is empty.

Fill the tank with gas and take a resistance measurement at the gauge. If the multimeter reads 8 to 12 ohms, the gauge is defective. If the resistance figure is way off, remove the sending unit (after you use most of the gas to facilitate the tank removal) and check resistance again by physically moving the float up and down to its maximum travel positions.

Before you go through all the diagnosis work, I would verify that you are indeed filling the tank to capacity when taking on gas; some tanks, depending on the filler necks, are difficult to fill completely.

Lights and Oil

I have a 1995 Dodge pickup with a Cummins engine. Is it normal for the oil-pressure light and gauge to register no oil pressure for at least two seconds after the engine starts? This not only happens when it has been days since it was started, but when it has only been 10 minutes.

Also, when I changed the oil filter at 3,000 miles, the oil filter was only ¾ full of oil. Is this a problem? The Dodge dealer here says the engine has no check valve so the oil dranks back into the pan after it sits a while. They checked the oil pressure at 35 psi at idle.

JAMES ROBERTS
TEXARKANA, TX

James, if the gauge registers good oil pressure within a couple of seconds, everything's working fine. Cummins engineers require that oil pressure is indicated on the gauge within 15 seconds. You'll find these instructions in the *Cummins Operation and Maintenance Manual B Series Engines* listed on pages 1–4.

Your oil-filter discovery is normal too. Since there is no check valve in the oil-filter housing, the oil will siphon back into the pan as the engine cools. If the engine is cold, the filter will not be full. I find this a positive feature allowing for a much cleaner procedure when changing the filter. If you change the filter when the engine is hot, expect the filter to be quite full; the oil will probably drip out around the seal as the filter is loosened, of course, making a mess.

Hot Manifolds

We are the owners of a 1987 Southwind Eagle, model 331 motorhome equipped with a Chevy 454 engine.

For more times than I care to think about, other motorhome owners tell me that we can expect major problems with the manifold setup on the engine.

The problem as I understand it seems to be the lack of gaskets and, that after 10,000 miles, we will be paying some exorbitant bills to correct the problems.

We have only 8,000 miles on our unit and have become more and more leery of using it for longer trips as a result of these discussions. Do we have a problem? If we do, what can be done about it in terms of preventative work?

LARRY AND SHIRLEY BOWMAN
MURRIETA, CA

First of all, I would not "ground" your motorhome because the exhaust manifolds may start to leak in the future. If they do develop a leak, you're not going to have a catastrophic failure and be stranded in the middle of nowhere. The noise from leaking exhaust manifolds can become fairly loud (and annoying) and after a while may create some engine damage, but you'll have plenty of notice.

The lack of gaskets is not the problem; there are none from the factory. The problem is excessive heat and the resultant warpage of the exhaust manifolds. If the exhaust manifolds do develop leaks, you can replace them with aftermarket headers (there are a number of companies supplying high-quality, heavy-duty headers for 454 engines in motorhomes) or you can replace them with Ring Manifolds. Ring makes replacement exhaust manifolds that are guaranteed for as long as you own the motorhome. The cost is $580 plus shipping. Included in the price are both exhaust manifolds, special copper gaskets and all the necessary hardware to make the installation. Ring Manifolds is at 210 Industrial Drive, Plymouth, MI 48170; (800) 233-3703.

Gas Tank Repairs

After reading July's "Tech Topics" column, I realized that I may have the answer to a problem Richard D. Golden has with his truck's gas tank. Enclosed is a brochure on Gas Tank Renu-USA, a company that specializes in repairing gas tanks.

> I happened to get this one in Iowa, but I'm sure the company
> has other applicators around the country.
>
> DONALD HILL
> BALLWIN, MO

Fuel-tank repairing has become a big topic in this column and we're
grateful to Don for leading us to a relatively new franchise that can
potentially help a lot of readers. The company is called Gas Tank Renu-
USA and there are currently 36 locations in the United States with
more on the way.

Gas Tank Renu-USA has a process that allows rebuilding of virtually any tank in any condition. Once the tank is taken to one of the repair facilities, the technician will defume it so that it can be worked
on safely. If you cannot find a local shop, then you can defume the
tank yourself prior to shipping.

To do so, simply add a couple of squirts of liquid dish soap to the
empty tank and continue to fill it with water until all the suds disap-
pear. Repeat the process and allow the tank to dry before shipping.

The process continues with sandblasting the entire surface to remove all rust and crud down to the bare metal. Then any holes are re-
paired. The inside of the tank is then coated with a wet, plastic material
that will adhere to the metal when cured. The outside is brushed with
a similar wet, plastic material and the entire tank is baked at 350–360°F
for curing.

According to company representatives, the process is very effective
and the end result is very attractive. As a matter of fact, they special-
ize in restoring tanks for custom cars and trucks. The process is backed
by a lifetime warranty on passenger-car and light-duty-truck tanks;
two years for all others.

The turnaround time is usually a day or two, depending on the
work load at the local shop. Of course, you'll need to add shipping
time both ways if you cannot find a local facility. The approximate
cost is $100-$500, depending on the size of the tank and the extent
of the damage.

You can contact the main office of Gas Tank Renu-USA at 12727
Greenfield, Detroit, MI 48227; (800) 932-2766.

Broken Bracket Bolt

I have a 29-foot Superior motorhome on a M-500 Dodge chassis, powered by a 440-3 engine. My problem is that the long alternator bolt has broken flush with the block (three times) and I have to use an EZ-out to remove the stub. I have checked the belt alignment with a straight edge and the belt appears to be running true.

My local Dodge dealer says "to buy extra bolts and spacers."

TOM MCLAUGHLIN
POST FALLS, ID

Tom, the broken bracket-bolt routine is common with the 440 engine. I've replaced a number of these bolts over the years using Chrysler's bolt kit, part no. 3549591. The kit consists of a grade 8, hardened bolt and the appropriate spacers. It even has instructions for installation. Typical off-the-shelf, hardware-store-grade bolts just don't cut the mustard.

I know the kit is still available because I ordered and received one from my local Dodge dealership at presstime. The cost should be around $18.30.

Early Birds

One of my pet campground peeves is the guy who starts his engine (usually a noisy diesel, but often a gasoline engine) at 6:30 in the morning and lets it run for a half hour to warm it up, disturbing all his neighbors in the process. I'm sure he feels he must do this to protect his engine. By all that I've read and heard on the subject, including what it says in my owners manual (I have a Ford diesel), this is not necessary and may, in fact, be harmful to the engine. My understanding is that the best way to warm an engine is to drive it at moderate speeds.

My owners manual says that after starting a cold engine, allow it to idle for approximately 15 seconds or until normal oil pressure reading is indicated. It also states, under cold weather operation: "Whenever possible, let the engine run for a few minutes to warm up before driving. However, the diesel engine generates very little excess heat at idle, and prolonged idling will not improve heater performance nor aid in initial cab warm-up. When you drive away, take it easy at first to give transmission and axle lubricants time to circulate."

It is my understanding that a two- or three-minute warm-up is all that is necessary (not 20 or 30, like so many do). Your comments on this subject would be appreciated.

JOHN H. SLEVIN
LIVINGSTON, TX

One of the worst disturbances in campgrounds nowadays is the diesel driver who gets up early to start warming up his engine. An hour or so later, after breakfast and chores, he unhooks and drives off, leaving everyone in the campground thoroughly awake. Just exactly how much warming up do those stinkpots require as compared to a gas engine?

ROY LUNDAY
ALPINE, CA

Gasoline engines should be run for approximately 20 seconds so that the oil can circulate adequately. Take it slow and easy until the engine reaches normal operating temperature. If you allow the engine to idle for a long time in order to reach operating temperature, you chance cylinder washdown (from unburnt fuel) because fuel vaporization is poor and combustion temperature is not optimum. Cylinder washdown removes the protective film of oil, allowing accelerated wear between the piston rings and cylinder walls.

Extended idling also is detrimental to diesel engines. After starting a diesel, wait about one minute to stabilize pressures and drive with a light touch on the throttle until the engine reaches normal operating temperature. In very cold temperatures, you may have to wait a few minutes. If the diesel is allowed to idle longer than necessary, unburnt fuel can wash the oil from the cylinder walls, creating the same problem as in gasoline engines. In both cases, driving slowly, under light load, is the best procedure for bringing the engine up to operating temperature.

The Other Diesel Fuel

We have a 1990 Dodge Cummins, with which we tow a 27-foot travel trailer. An acquaintance recently told me that he has friends who frequently use heating oil in their diesel engines. I'm rather skeptical of this, but I thought that I would ask the experts. Just what is the difference between No. 1 and No. 2 diesel and heating fuel, and what would be the effect of using such a fuel in a diesel engine? Would it harm the engine if it were used in an emergency?

ARTHUR P. RICKER
SHELTON, WA

Heating fuel is diesel fuel and it will work fine in your Cummins, as well as other diesel engines. As a matter of fact, it has a higher sulfur content that provides improved lubrication. But there is a big catch: It's illegal to use this stuff to fuel vehicles driven on any public road. To prevent cheating, the heating fuel is colored with a red dye. You're allowed to use this fuel as long as the vehicle is used off road—farm and ranch vehicles, etc.

If you get caught using the red-dyed fuel, you're in for a possible hefty fine. Vehicles are regularly tested for diesel-fuel misuse by local enforcement agencies. Of course, you may never get caught, but that's how most criminals think. The reason you can't use heating fuel on the highway is simply a matter of money—taxes. The federal government slaps a 24⅓-cent tax on each gallon of diesel; the states follow suit with taxes ranging from nine to 33 cents per gallon. Heating fuel is free of these taxes and, consequently, much cheaper.

Gooseneck and Ball

Could you tell me why makers of fifth-wheels do not use the gooseneck-and-ball hookup?

RAY ELLINGSON
MAY CITY, IA

The gooseneck-and-ball hookup is popular for use on horse and stock trailers; it's not commonly used on recreational fifth-wheels. Although it seems like a good idea because the pickup bed is virtually free of bulky hitch hardware, the hitching process may actually be more difficult. Lining up the gooseneck on the ball is especially difficult when towing with an extended-cab truck since the driver may have limited visibility to the hitch point. Also, the gooseneck hardware on the fifth-wheel looks unwieldy to many onlookers.

The equipment is available for those who prefer the gooseneck-and-ball setup. Many fifth-wheel manufacturers will accommodate prospective buyers and install optional gooseneck hitches. Balls—used to accept the gooseneck coupler that can be turned around, leaving the bed free when the fifth-wheel is not towed—can be installed. Also, for those who prefer not to cut a large hold in the bed of the truck, balls that can be mounted on conventional fifth-wheel-hitch bed rails are also available.

Straight Hitching

We recently bought a new Ford Explorer to pull our 2,700-pound Prowler trailer. I noticed that there is more sway with the trailer when large trucks pass us. We previously had an '87 Grand Wagoneer Jeep, and the problem was less noticeable.

I was told that the weight might not be evenly distributed. The hitch on the Explorer might not be level with the hitch of the trailer. Could you please send me any information on weight distribution.

ROLAND HOFFELDER
GARDEN CITY, NJ

Based on the weight you supplied, we'll figure that your trailer is in the 18- to 20-foot range, which is a good size for your Explorer. Short-wheel-base vehicles, like the Explorer, should not be used to tow trailers longer than 22 feet. Although the Explorer is rated to tow heavier trailers, it should only be used to tow 22-footers when they are evenly balanced.

Balance is very important when towing with the Explorer. For example, if a 30-gallon water tank is in the front of the trailer, hitch weight can vary 200 pounds, depending on water level. If proper hitch weight (approximately 12 percent of gross weight) is dependent on a full water tank, then obviously, an empty tank will affect handling. On the other hand, if the tank is in the very rear of the trailer, the water (depending on level) can act as a pendulum, shifting the weight laterally, again affecting handling. When packing the trailer, try to balance the load, front to back and side to side.

Proper hitching is also important. An equalizing hitch will not do its intended job if it is not adjusted properly. Start with a level trailer. If the street or driveway is flat, measure each corner of the trailer, making adjustments in attitude until it is level.

Measure the distance from the inside of the coupler on the end of the trailer A-frame to the ground. Now install the ball mount into the receiver on the Explorer. Adjust the ball height (top of the ball to ground) until it is about an inch higher than the coupler measurement.

Measure the distance from the top edge of each tow-vehicle wheel well to the ground; record these figures. Hitch up the trailer and adjust the tension of the spring bars; the amount of drop at each wheel well should be equal. If it is, and the trailer is relatively level, then approximately 50 percent of the hitch weight will be distributed to the front axle of the tow vehicle and trailer axles (approximately 25 percent each).

Although the hitch may be adjusted perfectly, the trailer may still be susceptible to sway; it's the nature of the beast with short-wheel-base vehicles. But you can limit sway by installing a friction-type sway control. That's the sliding device that is attached to a second (smaller) ball on the ball mount and to another ball attached to the trailer A-frame. This will help considerably.

The sway you feel when being overtaken by large, fast-moving trucks can also be squelched by activating the trailer brakes momentarily (using the brake controller lever). If you do all the above and resist overloading the trailer, your towing experiences should be very enjoyable and safe.

Bearing Disaster

While traveling on a winding road, generally at speeds less than 45 mph, the wheel bearings on the left rear wheel of my 26-foot fifth-wheel disintegrated. The resulting friction caused sufficient heat to melt the plastic hub cover. The wheel was ready to come off the axle. Fortunately, a motorist behind me saw the wheel wobbling and got me to stop before that occurred.

Inspection showed that there was plenty of grease; the roller retainer had broken and the rollers were loose in the grease; the spindle nut and cotter pin were in place, and the brake system and wheel drum were damaged beyond repair. The wheels had been packed 5,356 miles before the incident. To be safe, I had new bearings installed on all four wheels and had new brakes and a drum installed on the left rear wheel.

Not long after the repairs, the bearings on the left rear wheel failed again. This time I stopped; the bearings, seals, spindle nut and cotter pin were all missing. There was no grease, although it appeared that the grease had been sprayed out on the wheel. The wheel was completely free on the axle and was taken off without having to remove any nuts. Apparently, it had been held on by the wheel drum grabbing the brake shoes. The rubber on the inner edge of the tire had worn off as if the wheel was not rotating before I stopped. The axle was damaged beyond repair. It appeared to be slightly bent. Before the incident, I thought the rear left wheel didn't look as if it was vertical—the bottom seemed to be out. But I thought it was an optical illusion. I had been traveling several hundred miles at speeds between 60 and 70 mph; the wheels were packed 9,350 miles before the latest incident.

CHARLES F. HALL
LOS ALTOS, CA

Based on your description, I have to believe that the bearing was not preloaded properly during the first service you mentioned. If bearings are not preloaded to manufacturer's specifications, then the excess grease will not be removed from between the rollers, resulting in too much wheelbearing play. It's also important to use the right type of high-temperature grease when packing the bearings and to make sure the grease is forced between each roller.

If the bearings are jiggling around, excess friction can create tremendous heat and damage the axle/wheel/brake components. I suspect that the spindle was bent during the first incident—that's why you noticed the wheel out of kilter and experienced the second failure. It probably was not an optical illusion and should have been inspected at that time. The adverse tire wear was also an indication that the wheel was out of whack. I recently inspected a trailer axle with a similar problem and the heat was so great that the bearings and races were ground to minute pieces, the wheel burned as if someone used a blow torch and the spindle bent severely. The only fix was to replace the axle and all the wheel/brake components

If you service the bearings regularly and properly, you should be able to travel trouble-free. Most axle manufacturers recommend repacking the bearings every 12,000 miles. That's good advice. Preload specifications vary, but Dexter, for example, recommends tightening the spindle nut to 50 lbs.-ft. on its 2,000-to-8,000-pound-rated trailer axles. The spindle nut is then loosened to remove the preload torque and finger tightened until snug. The nut is then secured with a cotter pin in the first nut castelation that lines up with the hole in the spindle.

Air Springs

The air springs on my 1993 Class A Chevy 454 have regularly lost pressure since they were new 20,000 miles ago. At first, the loss was 2 to 4 pounds per week. Recently I took it out of a three-month storage and the bags had no pressure. I filled them to 80 pounds the night before leaving, but the next morning they were down to 50 pounds. I refilled them and drove 400 miles, but the next morning they were empty. This pattern continued over the next few days, and each day the loss was a little less. After a week, the loss was down to just a pound or two each day.

I have an air-bag extension-hose system installed (metal fittings with hard plastic hoses) that terminates at a pressure monitor where the bags can be filled. All fittings are tight.

Are Chevy air springs prone to slow leaks that require filling every few days or do I have a problem? I have heard that there is a replacement bag available that retains pressure over a longer period of time. Do you know about it?

ROGER VESTAL
EVERGREEN, CO

I own a 1981 Itasca 26-foot Class A that has air bags in the coil springs up front; one has ruptured. I understand that it is expensive to replace these bags. Is there an alternative to these bags, such as heavy-duty shocks, or can I let the air out of the good one and run the rig without them?

JOHN ZWICKER
WILMINGTON, MA

Air-spring leaks or ruptures are usually caused by improper inflation. If these bags are not kept nominally filled, they can develop leaks or even ruptures by rubbing against the springs. There is no way to fix a leak—the bags must be replaced—and you cannot run without them since these air springs are designed to increase the load capacity of the front axle. If you remove them, the front suspension will probably bottom out, which can cause damage to other suspension components. There is no aftermarket hardware that can be used in lieu of air springs.

Replacing the OEM air springs does take quite a bit of effort and, most likely, cannot be accomplished by shade-tree mechanics. And they are very expensive to boot. Firestone offers a replacement air bag, called Coil Right, that is designed to be installed easily and is protected by a lifetime warranty.

The leak-path potential increases with the use of extension fill systems. If you determine that the air bags are not leaking, you should scrutinize the hoses and fittings in the extension kit. Checking the bags for leaks will probably require removal and immersion in water, if the hole(s) is not obvious.

Chevrolet recommends that at least 10 psi be maintained to avoid chafing and that under load the bags are inflated to 50 psi (for the 5,000-pound-rated axle).

Air-Bag Replacements

Regarding the air-springs letter in the June issue, I take exception to your answer, "There is no aftermarket hardware that can be used in lieu of air springs." We own a 1994 Bounder on a Chevy chassis and we've always hated the hassle and handling problems from air springs. After talking to numerous RV repair shops, we kept getting the same advice: Install SuperCoil springs.

Our Bounder finally rides level with no front-end sag. We have a softer ride and the handling is much better. We no longer have to fill air bags. SuperCoil was the best investment we've made. No air bags to replace in the future.

TERRY R. LESTER
BULLHEAD CITY, AZ

Although there may be a number of GM-chassis owners out there who use these aftermarket springs and experience no failures, Chevrolet cautions against their use. Here's exactly what Chevrolet says: "GM recommends the use of only factory-approved replacement parts for this 'safety-sensitive' area of the vehicle. Some aftermarket coils are physically too large for the normally designed working area of the front coil spring as the wheel goes through its ride travel. On crush, these aftermarket springs can create a metal-to-metal 'coil-bound' condition before the ride stops come into play. (The damage created by using a metal-to-metal solid coil can be compared to installing a piece of well casing in place of a spring, then raising the vehicle in the air and dropping the vehicle to the ground.) The force of this metal-to-metal 'coil-bound' condition is transferred directly into the potential destruction of the lower ball joints or broken lower control arms."

Obviously, based on GM's warnings, we opted not to recommend these springs. Approved replacement coil springs should be installed only by a qualified service technician.

Leave it Running

I recently traded my standard-shift Dodge D-50 pickup for a 1995 Ford Taurus LX with an automatic shift. I heard that for short trips you can leave the ignition on and the engine running and safety tow this vehicle with four wheels on the ground without damaging the transmission.

RICHARD JONES
GREELEY, CO

Richard, you *can* leave the engine running to achieve transmission lubrication, but there are too many drawbacks in doing so. If the engine dies while being towed behind your motorhome, you're in big trouble. And you probably won't discover that it quit running until it's too late.

The other factor is the increased engine wear due to extended idling. Allowing your engine to idle, especially when the fuel vaporization and combustion temperatures are not ideal, can cause increased cylinder washdown, which accelerates wear. When allowed to idle, the fuel is not burned completely; this unburned fuel washes the oil from the cylinder walls, creating more friction and accelerated ring and liner wear. Extended idling also allows excessive compression blow-by that contaminates the engine oil.

I suggest that if you plan on towing the Taurus, you modify the car so it can be towed without the engine running. For information regarding the proper modifications, contact Remco 15 4138 S. 89th St., Omaha, NE 68127; (800) 228-2481.

Honda (and Ford) Towing

Exactly what determines whether a vehicle can be towed with all four wheels on the ground without using a tow dolly? I have talked to Honda dealers, Ford dealers, transmission specialists and my own mechanic about towing my 1991 Honda Civic or 1991 Ford Festiva with a manual transmission behind my motorhome without using a tow dolly.

The Honda dealer said, "Oh no! You'll ruin the transmission. And there is nothing that you can do to your automobile to make it towable on all four wheels." Ford said, "It can't be done. The transmission will run backward. You either have to use a tow dolly or purchase a vehicle that is specially designed to tow with all four wheels on the ground." My transmission specialist said, "I don't see why you can't. It's not an automatic that needs lubrication pumped to the transmission. Just make sure the key is turned to unlock the wheels so that they will turn freely. If an alteration does need to be made, we don't know what it would be." And, finally, my mechanic said, "Gee, I really don't know."

JOHN G. GRIFFIN JR.
WOODBRIDGE, VA

I would like to tow my 1995 Honda Accord, 2.2-liter engine with automatic transmission behind my motorhome. I would like to get your feelings on this. Have you had any bad reports on towing this model car?

CHARLES S. DUNN
ARROYO GRANDE, CA

The most important concern is whether or not towing on all fours will damage the transmission. In many cases, the turning of the driveshaft—even though the car has a manual transmission and the shifter is in Neutral—can damage internal parts because of a lack of proper lubrication. It's hard for many owners to realize that just because the transmission is in Neutral doesn't mean that the internal components are not turning. In some cases, the oil pump is operated while the vehicle is being towed.

Keep in mind, though, many vehicles can be made towable with driveshaft modifications, like those marketed by Remco. You can contact Remco at 4138 S. 89th St., Omaha, NE 68127; (800) 228-2481.

Now let's get to the nitty gritty. You should be able to tow your Festiva with a manual transmission with no problems. When the 1991 model came out, the owner's manual specified that it could not be towed on all four wheels. But Ford announced shortly after that the Festiva could be towed and that engineers were making changes to the owner's manual. Yours might even have the latest information.

Many people tow Hondas without problems, but the company has never "officially" sanctioned towing on all four wheels. Once in a while I hear from someone who had a breakdown due to towing, but usually the problem can be traced to owner error, like forgetting to put the transmission in Neutral. Honda did, though, announce the proper procedure for placing automatic transmissions in Neutral, even though they still did not recommend towing. The procedure is as follows: Make sure the transmission fluid level is full, start the engine, shift the lever from Park to Drive, then shift the lever from Drive to Neutral. Turn off the engine and make sure the steering wheel is unlocked. It's important not to place the shift lever into Neutral directly from Park.

Incidentally, Honda has recently announced that its 1997 CR-V can be towed dinghy-style without experiencing drivetrain damage. You must follow the above shifting procedures and make sure you stop every 200 miles (while towing), start the engine and run the shift lever through all the gears. Make sure you remember to again place the lever in Neutral using the proper procedure.

Towing an Explorer

Several months ago we purchased a 1995 Ford Explorer with automatic transmission and automatic Control Trac 4WD. Prior to purchase we were told by a Ford salesperson, and verified by reading the owners manual, that this vehicle was equipped with a Neutral Tow Kit that would allow it to be towed on all four wheels with no restrictions on speed or distance. This was very important to us because towability was a prime criteria in our purchase.

To use this feature, the manual states that the vehicle should be taken to a Ford dealer where a procedure would be performed to activate it. When we tried to have this done, we were told that Ford had put a temporary hold on the procedure because of technical problems, but that they were developing a fix. We have checked with the selling dealer several times since then and have always been told the same story.

In checking with other Ford dealers, however, we get different and inconsistent stories, some saying that the feature is not and never will be operable. I have on two separate occasions called Ford's customer-service center in an attempt to get further information, but in both cases was told that they had no information on the subject. A letter to Ford produced equally noncommittal and unsatisfactory results. Meanwhile we have been unable to tow the Explorer as we intended.

DAVID GOSS
COSTA MESA, CALF.

In a bulletin issued by Ford, 4-wheel-drive Explorers with the electronic transfer-case control built after Dec. 1, 1995, can be fitted with a Neutral Tow Kit. This kit can be installed by a local Ford dealer and should cost around $115 for parts and labor. When installed, the Neutral Tow Kit allows the Explorer to be towed behind a motorhome with all four wheels on the ground and no speed or distance restrictions.

The kit, which works in harmony with a computer module and harness installed at the factory after Dec. 1, 1995, can only be fitted to Explorers equipped with the 4.0-liter engine, automatic transmission and 4x4 transfer case. It will not be available for Explorers equipped with the 5.0-liter engine and 2-wheel drives. According to the bulletin, the kit cannot be used on Explorers built before Dec. 1, 1995.

The owners manual will include instructions for using this feature; there will be an indicator light under the instrument panel that illuminates when the system is activated. Owners who have Explorers built before Dec. 1, 1995, are encouraged to follow the previous instructions for towing with the electronic 4x4 control—in other words, it is not towable on all four wheels without driveline modifications.

Jiffy Tow

I am trying to get some information on what was called a Jiffy Tow back in the 1980s. This lifted the dinghy vehicle with a boat-reel type of hoist onto the hitch ball of the motorhome, allowing the dinghy vehicle to be towed on two wheels—much like a regular trailer.

ROLAND L. MORIN
DAPHNE, AL

Roland, Jiffy Tow has not been around for many years—and that's good. Unfortunately, many RVers thought that this device was a pretty good idea, eliminating the need for tow bars and dollies. But, in practice, the dinghy vehicle presented way too much hitch weight on the rear of the motorhome. The problem is actually two-fold: Most motorhome frames are not designed to carry the weight of a car's front end, and weight distribution is thrown way off when that much weight is slapped on the far rear of the motorhome. Overloading of the rear axle is also a serious concern and handling characteristics can be changed for the worse. Stick to a tow bar or dolly.

Fudge Factor

I am getting ready to buy my first trailer and tow vehicle and I have a question about weights and the law. The dealers are telling me that on both the trailer and tow vehicle—if I am over the gross vehicle weight rating—there is a 20% to 30% safety factor. I don't know if this is true or not; I am looking at 20,000 pounds for the gross combination weight. If this is true, am I legal if the vehicle(s) is licensed properly? If it is not legal, will I be liable if I'm involved in an accident for exceeding the limits of the trailer?

JAMES F. HOLLAND
WHEELING, IL

Federal law requires that all manufacturers of vehicles used on public roads provide the gross vehicle weight rating (gvwr), gross axle weight rating (gawr) for each axle and the tire capacities. Membership in the Recreation Vehicle Industry Association (RVIA) requires that manufacturers provide the unloaded vehicle weight (uvw) and the net carrying capacity beginning with 1997 models. The uvw includes the factory-installed options and full LP gas. This weight does not include fuel, freshwater or accessories installed by the dealer. Net carrying capacity reflects the weight of all the passengers (if applicable), supplies, water and LP gas and is determined by subtracting the uvw from the gvwr.

The new weight-labeling system allows the manufacturer to use "approximate" weights, which suggests that it's still prudent to weigh vehicles if an overload is suspected. This is especially true if the trailer you are looking to buy may be heavier than the weight allowed by the manufacturer of the tow vehicle.

There are no "published" fudge factors. The maximum weights listed by the individual manufacturer are based on a number of variables, including tire capacity, axle capacity, frame strength, brakes, engine, etc. These figures are provided to enhance safety; there's no law that states that you cannot tow a trailer that's too heavy for the truck. As far as legalities in the event of an accident, you should consult a lawyer for that information. If you overload the vehicle, you may be looking at premature wear and tear that could be costly down the road.

Although there are many RVers out there towing trailers that are too heavy for the tow vehicle and reporting no adverse damage or mechanical problems, we suggest that you heed the manufacturer's weight specifications.

Need Towing Stability

In January we purchased a new 1850 Aljo Deluxe trailer that has a gross dry weight of about 3,273 pounds. The trailer is towed by a 1994 Ford Explorer with a trailer tow package rated at 5,500 pounds. We are using an Eaz-Lift weight-distributing hitch, but I am experiencing some instability. When I encounter a large slab-sided truck or bus, there is a pretty strong pull to the side as it approaches and passes. Also, I've found that I must keep very "still" steering when driving down curves in the mountains.

What suggestions do you have? Do I need to install a sway-control device? If so, which type would give the best results?

JOHN BARKMAN
SOUTH PASADENA, CA

The feeling of instability you get when being passed by large trucks is normal. What you are feeling is the bow wave created by the vehicle as it overtakes you from the rear. How much correction is needed to restabilize is dependent upon the balance of the trailer and proper adjustment of the hitch. With short-wheelbase vehicles like yours, it's important that the hitch weight is at least 10 to 12 percent of the total weight of the trailer.

You can control some of the trailer's fishtailing by installing a friction-type sway control. These devices attach to small balls, one mounted on the ball mount and one on the trailer A-frame. There are a number of quality devices on the market available at any RV supply store.

Make sure the hitch is adjusted properly. If you have too much weight on the rear, because the spring bars are not cinched up tight enough, there could be some unloading of the front axle. I suspect that is what is causing that "squirrely" feeling when negotiating curves. When adjusting the hitch, make sure there is equal drop in the front and rear of the tow vehicle. You can measure the distance between the ground (flat surface) and the wheel well before you hitch up and confirm the drop after the spring-bar chains are secured in the brackets. If there is more drop in the front than the rear, the spring bars are too tight; if the front becomes unloaded, the spring bars are too loose.

If you get into a serious sway situation, whether from winds, road-surface irregularities or large passing trucks, you should always be ready to manually activate the brake controller without using the tow vehicle's brakes. This will dramatically help to stabilize uncontrolled lateral movements.

Real Heavy Towing

I'm looking to buy a fairly large, heavy travel trailer that has a tongue weight of 1,300 pounds. My dealer would like to order this trailer for me, but he is afraid that I will not be able to find a hitch that is rated high enough to do the job.

I appreciate my dealer's concern, but I do not want a fifth-wheel trailer. What's the best solution?

T. ANDERSON
DALLAS, TX

Until recently, you would have to exceed all the manufacturer's ratings for weight-distributing hitches. Class IV hitches are rated at 10,000 pounds trailer weight with 1,000-pound maximum hitch weight. Interest in large, conventional trailers seems to be on the rise, especially with the availability of slide-outs.

Reese Products has introduced a line of heavy-duty Class V hitches marketed under the Titan nameplate designed to meet the needs of those interested in these mega travel trailers. The new receivers and weight-distributing hitches are rated to handle 14,000 pounds trailer weight and up to 1,700 pounds hitch weight. Reese has receiver applications for many late-model, full-size pickups, vans and, of course, the Suburban.

The company has achieved the higher rating by using a 3½-inch receiver cross tube and a 2½-inch receiver (box) opening. You should be able to find this equipment at your local dealer. For additional information you can write Reese Products, 51671 State Road 19 N., Elkhart, IN 46514, or call its tech line at (800) 758-0869.

Too Tall to Tow?

I want to buy a four-wheel-drive truck to pull a fifth-wheel. I am looking for a Ford extended cab, 460-cid, four-speed automatic with overdrive, 4.10 rear end, ¾-ton pickup. The fifth-wheels we want are either 27 or 29 feet with a slide-out, and weigh 8,000–10,000 pounds.

I was told by one dealer that he could not put his fifth-wheel behind a four-wheel-drive truck since there would not be enough clearance between the cabover and the truck rails without reversing the shackles on the springs of the fifth-wheel.

Some other people have said we could remove the block from between the springs and axle of the truck to lower the bed of the truck. I am afraid of what that would to to the suspension.

The measurements I made on a friend's two-wheel-drive Ford pickup showed only 2 inches less height than the dealer specs of the four-wheel-drive Ford truck. I also talked to other dealers about it and they said I could pull any of their rigs with a four-wheel-drive truck.

DAVID SLYKHUIS
TEMPLE CITY, CA

Most ¾-ton four-wheel-drive pickups can be used to tow the majority of fifth-wheels on the market. There are some fifth-wheels, though, that are too low and may need to be lifted. This is done by changing the position of the spring pack, commonly called "reversing the axles."

You may find a few more fifth-wheels that are too low for 1-ton four-wheel drives. It's usually not a problem for Chevrolet trucks; some Dodges and Fords have taller profiles. Trucks with heavier springs (higher gross axle weight ratings) are usually taller. If you modify the suspension, you're defeating the purpose of buying a truck with a higher capacity.

At minimum, you should have 5 inches of clearance between the bottom of the cabover and the top of the bed (cargo box). It would be better to have 6 ½–7 inches of clearance. If you like the trailer and it's a little low for your truck, and the hitch and/or pin box on the trailer cannot be adjusted to allow for the proper amount of clearance, don't hesitate in having a professional repair facility modify the placement of the fifth-wheel axles. At worst, you might have to add another step for easier doorway accessibility.

Flipping the Axles

I have a 1972 Terry 22-foot travel trailer, and as you know, those early trailers were built quite low and drag pretty easily when traveling in and out of dips such as those in gas station driveways. Before I retired, we just used the trailer occasionally and lived with the inconvenience. Now that we use it more often, I want to know if I would run into any great problem by putting the axles on top of the springs. This would give me about 2 inches more clearance, which would be a great benefit.

J. REX RECORD
AUSTIN, CO

Reversing or flipping the axles is a common practice for improving ground clearance. Most RV dealer service centers can handle the job. It entails removing the axles and installing new spring pads. The axles are then rebolted to the bottom side of the springs using new U-bolts and nuts. It's critical that the axles are aligned properly to prevent adverse tire wear and poor handling. The entire job should run around $140, including the necessary parts.

Turning Sharp with a Fifth-wheel

We have a 1989 King of the Road fifth-wheel, 36-foot with a 4-wheel chassis. On a couple of trips where we had to do some backing to park; we've had to make some very sharp turns. When we've done this, I've been able to see the trailer's wheels, and it seems like the turn is so sharp that the tires are ready to pop off the rims.

What harm am I doing to the tires, the chassis? What are the immediate dangers of too sharp of a turn? Could I break bearings, split a wheel, or even tip the chassis from the trailer body? Please help.

CHARLES HAFERMAN
AURORA, CO

Turning a fifth-wheel sharply is one of the features many owners appreciate. When making a radical turn to maneuver into a tight spot, the tires are not able to follow the chassis. That's because the axles have no steering capability. Therefore the tires look as if they are coming off the rims. While there is nothing dangerous with making sharp turns, it's best to avoid them (pivoting the truck completely on the kingpin) because it increases tire wear due to scrubbing. In hot weather, turning sharply can damage asphalt paving if the trailer is on the heavy side.

After making such a turn, pull the trailer straight ahead or back it up until the wheels return to a normal state visually. If you allow the wheels to remain bound up and unhitch, it's possible that the trailer will surge forward (or backward), causing possible injury, especially if you place the landing gear on blocks.

Manual Transmissions

I am considering changing to a fifth-wheel and I have questions about the tow vehicle. I have seen numerous articles on automatic transmission care, problems and precautions. I have yet to see any articles on stick shifts.

I am leaning toward a Dodge diesel but am undecided whether to get a stick or an automatic.

DEAN R. LANTRIP
OROVILLE, CALIF.

One of the reasons you don't read much about manual transmissions for serious towing is because most of the manufacturers rate their trucks to tow heavier trailers with automatics. The problem has always been that people tend to burn clutches when towing heavy loads—a problem that doesn't exist with automatic transmissions.

This, however, is not the case with 1994-98 Dodge trucks equipped with the Cummins turbo-diesel engine. The tow ratings for these trucks with manual transmissions are equal to the same trucks with automatic transmissions.

Your Dodge dealer has a towing guide to help you select the correct engine, transmission and axle-ratio combination capable of handling the weight of your trailer. Make sure you know the actual trailer weight. If you don't, take it to a commercial scale and weigh it. If you rely solely on manufacturer-advertised weights, you might make a mistake when equipping your new truck.

LeSharo Believers

After coming up empty with a solution to finding an engine replacement for the LeSharos and Phasars, we got a number of letters from readers with possible drivetrain swaps. Here's one that looks pretty good:

There are a few Winnebago LeSharos and Itasca Phasars on the road that have been converted to the GM 3800, 6-cylinder engine. I am now driving a 1986 Phasar, which originally was powered by a Renault turbocharged diesel. My unit is now powered by a GM 3800 engine, salvaged from a 1991 Oldsmobile.

After removing the Renault engine and drivetrain (including steering column), struts and even some of the mounting boxes welded to the frame, the 3800 will fit very nicely. Very few adaptors were used; maybe four or five items were fabricated or altered. We wanted to keep everything either Phasar or Oldsmobile.

The most complicated part of the job was changing the wiring. To make the engine, instrument panel, and any accessories operational, we had to remove all the wiring from the Olds and install it in the Itasca. Olds wheels, hubs and brakes were also installed on the rear axle.

The coach was not modified except for the wheels, therefore, it still looks like a 1986 Itasca Phasar. But to drive it is a whole new experience. It must have twice the power; it can stay with any traffic on the interstates, it will tow my small pickup truck with ease, it's a delight to drive and I still get 15 mpg while towing and up to 20 mpg while cruising solo.

ELDON BANKSON
PIQUA, OH

Thanks, Eldon, we appreciate the information. From the number of letters we got regarding this subject, there's a real need for mechanics like this gentleman.

Interior and Exterior

Marker Light Mystery

Will you please tell me why RVs have marker lights? I see no reason for them. Why are they not on cars? I am against them because they all leak—at least they have on every RV that I have owned. I think some light maker got his foot in the door if it's the law. I can count on one hand how many times I have used them. They are cheaply made and cause many leaks.

ROY ST. JOHN
ANGOLA, N.Y.

Marker lights, and in some cases reflectors, are required on all vehicles that are more than 80 inches in width. The number, location and spacing is specified by *Federal Motor Vehicle Safety Standard No. 108.*

Many of these marker lights are cheaply made and do leak. Some of these lights, especially the older versions, have very primitive bulb bases. The light bulbs are grounded though the sidewall and a hot (12-volt DC) wire is pressed into a slot. These fixtures typically leak or build condensation. Thus, the wire connection corrodes and the light bulb fails to light. In some cases, poor fixture sealing results in water leakage inside the walls of the RV.

Roy, if you want to end this frustration, purchase the marker light fixtures that have sealed bulb bases. They are fairly well made and, if sealed properly against the sidewall, should provide a leak-free environment for the RV as well as the marker light. I use the No. 59 marker lights made by Bargman. They usually sell for $3.59 and are available at most RV parts stores.

Molding Burning

We have a 1989 30-foot Southwind motorhome and the vinyl moldings along the sides, front and top edge are turning brown or rust color in spots. What can be done about this?

S.C. WOLFENBARGER
ONTARIO, CA

The brown color is due to direct exposure to sunlight. The sun is actually burning the molding, giving it a brownish—ugly—look. Once the molding is burned, it's time for replacement; there are no treatments to bring the material back to its original condition.

You can prolong this repair by treating the molding monthly with a coat of a good protectant, like 303. The protectant closes the pores of the molding, resisting the sun's strong rays. Fortunately, this molding is rather cheap and easy to replace. If you can shelter the rig from the sun's rays, you'll also be miles ahead.

Rubber-Roof Chalking

I have a 1989 Travel Master Class C that has a rubber roof. I have trouble with chalking or oxidizing, or whatever the proper term is. When it rains, this is a problem because it runs onto my driveway. Is there a maintenance routine I can use to prevent this?

CARL KNELLY
BERWICK, PA

The rubber-roof issue seems to be one of the most popular topics among our readers, and rightly so. Approximately 96 percent of all new RVs have EPDM rubber roofs. You know the old joke about death and taxes; well now there is a third fact of RV life that's certain: Membrane-type roofs will experience some degree of weathering during their lifetime. The white stuff you're seeing is a product of oxidation due to prolonged exposure to the sun and other elements.

Unless you can store your rig inside a garage or keep it covered, you may have to deal with chalking. The degree of chalking is dependent on a number of factors, including the consistency of the chemicals used in the mixing process, the type of chemicals used and, very importantly, where the rig is stored geographically. Some roofs may never have a chalking problem. Unfortunately, there is no way to know that before buying the RV.

Although EPDM roofs are warranted 10 to 12 years, the owner is responsible for performing adequate maintenance procedures. White streaks running down the sidewalls look terrible but, with a little care, can be controlled.

If you have this chalking problem, you'll need to scrub off a very thin (minute, as a matter of fact) top layer of the rubber roof. Using a medium to stiff brush and a cleaner like Boraxo, scrub the entire surface of the roof (using plenty of water, of course) until the white, powdery substance is completely gone. The grit in the cleaner will remove the weathered part; you can test the roof by wiping your hand over the rubber after it is completely dry. Repeat the process until your hands no longer show chalk. It is very important that you rinse the roof thoroughly after scrubbing.

Don't worry about scrubbing your roof away; the amount you are removing is hardly measurable. You may have to perform this task every year, but that's normal and your roof will last for a very long time.

By contrast, if the white chalking returns in a month or so, you have a chronic problem and you'll have to treat the roof to control the oxidation. In this case, after initial scrubbing, coat the clean roof with a protectant such as Protect All or 303. Unfortunately, you'll have to continue these treatments for the life of your roof if you want it to look nice.

While these rubber roofs have been specially formulated for exposure to sun and other elements, they do have to be cleaned periodically, even if they do not show signs of chalking. Dirt, tree sap, the effects of acid rain and other debris can make these roofs look rather dingy, detracting from the overall nice looks of your RV. You should consider a thorough cleaning at least four times a year; monthly is even better.

Use a medium-bristle brush and a mild laundry detergent with water to clean the roof. Again, make sure you rinse until all the residue is gone. Household bleach can be allowed to soak into small stubborn-stain areas, but is must be rinsed thoroughly. Do not use any cleaners containing petroleum distillates or that are citric based. Only use abrasives for the process explained above and, even then, do not use overly harsh abrasive cleaners.

So there you have it. Rubber roofs are warranted against defects for a long time, but they will not stay clean on their own. If you want your rig to be shiny clean, take the time to maintain your rubber roof, even thought most of the surface is out of sight.

Finish is History

Our 1984 27-foot Overland motorhome has a severe amount of chalking on the all-fiberglass skin. We have tried several types of fiberglass cleaner, but to no avail. Nature's elements have turned the finish to a dull color. I would appreciate any advice you could give me in restoring the shine and protecting the finish.

JIM NORRIS
OKMULGEE, OK

Once the gelcoat finish is gone, there's really nothing you can use to restore the original luster. You have a couple of options: The fiberglass skin can be refinished with new gelcoat material. The gelcoat should be mixed with the original color of the exterior. Another method is to have the surface prepared and painted in the color of your choice. Use good-quality automotive paint.

Once you restore the finish, you should treat the surface with a protectant. The sun and nature's elements are hard on fiberglass. I found that 303 works real well and, if you repeat the process every month or two, the exterior will continue to look nice. There are a number of automotive and marine waxes on the market that will also protect the finish, although waxing is more labor intensive. Of course, you could also protect the motorhome with a good-quality cover.

Imron Paint

Reading through an ad list, I came across the name Imron when describing the paint. Do you know what it is and can it be bought and used by a handyman like me?

JESSE E. HALL
SPRING HILL, FL

Imron was one of the first polyurethane paints on the market. In the old days, it was more common to see airplanes painted with Imron than cars because of the high cost. Today there are a number of polyurethane paints available, but they are still more expensive than your typical automotive paint. For example, the average car paint job with Imron could be $300-$500 more. But, of course, that depends on the area and the individual body/paint shop.

Unfortunately, Jesse, Imron and the similar polyurethane paints are not designed to be applied by the do-it-yourselfer. This paint is very temperamental when applying and, more importantly, you must be protected by a properly ventilated paint booth. Leave this to the professionals.

Airstream Shine

I have a 1988 27-foot Airstream trailer with a finish problem. The clear coat has come off in spots on the roadside above the windows; otherwise the finish is in excellent condition.

According to the Airstream factory and the local dealer, nothing can be done to improve the appearance of the skin (such as polishing or buffing). I would appreciate any ideas regarding cleaning up these oxidized areas prior to having the trailer stripped and recoated.

GEORGE F. DAVIS
WINSTON-SALEM, NC

The plasticoat material Airstream uses to enhance the luster of the aluminum finish has been specially formulated. Since aluminum has a high coefficient of expansion, most other coating materials will eventually become brittle and crack due to the aluminum's surface movement. High coefficient of expansion means that there is a lot of movement as the trailer exterior surface heats and cools with ambient-temperature changes.

There is a procedure for stripping the old plasticoat and refinishing the surface with new material, but some of the chemicals needed to do the job are harsh and should only be used by professionals. There are a number of dealers in the country who are qualified to do this procedure. You can locate the nearest dealer by calling Airstream at (513) 596-6111.

Since the plasticoat used by Airstream is somewhat softer than other automotive finishes, you should not use abrasive polishes or cleaning solvents, such as automatic dishwasher detergents or acid-etch cleaners. Acid-etch cleaners are dangerous to use and should only be handled by professionals.

The plasticoat starts to peel off the surface because the material loses its flexibility as it ages and becomes bleached out by the sun. This stuff is not permanent and life expectancy depends on environmental conditions. It's important to reapply the plasticoat before the aluminum surface has a chance to oxidize. Once the aluminum oxidizes, it is impossible to restore the finish to original condition. If you buff the surface, it will become brighter than the original satin finish and, unless you do the entire trailer, the exterior will look blotchy.

Clean your Airstream in the shade when the surface is cool. Use a mild, nonabrasive cleaner, rinse thoroughly and dry with a soft cloth or chamois to prevent spotting. It should be waxed with a good grade of nonabrasive automotive wax every six months. Make sure you remove bugs, sap and tar as soon as possible and rewax the surface.

Stubborn Stickers

I have a little problem and would appreciate your help. My motorhome is a Mobile Traveler made out of fiberglass and there are some stickers on the outside, similar to the Good Sam decal. It has been impossible to remove them. They seem to have been on since the rig was new (1984). Help.

J. SIEVERS
MIDWAY, GA

Removing stickers from RV exterior walls can be frustrating at best. Most stickers use a contact-type cement that can be released by applying heat. Use a hair dryer or heat gun (the tool designed for this purpose) to soften the sticker and work underneath it with a nylon or plastic putty knife; metal tools will create gouging and scratching. Be careful not to apply too much heat or you could delaminate the fiberglass if your walls are so constructed.

After removing most of the sticker, use denatured alcohol to eliminate any of the adhesive that remains on the surface. Denatured alcohol is one of the safest chemicals you can use for this purpose. Next, rub out the area with a mild liquid polishing compound, followed by an application of a good fiberglass wax (or equivalent product) to protect the surface. If the heat gun does not work, you can sand off the sticker and recondition the surface, but this should be done by a professional who knows how to handle gel-coated and Filon-fiberglass products. If you do happen to scratch a small area by accident, try using 600-grit wet/dry sandpaper under a very light touch, then rub out with polishing compound and wax (or use a protectant on) the surface.

Now remember, you're not allowed to use any of the above procedures to remove a Good Sam decal.

Retractable Step

We have a Kwikee retractable step, model 25005, on our motorhome and are experiencing the problem of the steps not retracting all the way. They have to be helped the last few inches or they will hang up a bit. I keep the steps well lubricated, but that does not seem to help. I see no limit switch that can be adjusted. The limit must be determined by the current draw of the motor, otherwise I believe the steps must go up all the way.

CALVIN J. MCNAMEE
SEATTLE, WA

Calvin, the fix should be easy. The head of the rivet that holds the linkage arm to the swivel ball may become bent down and catch or drag on the lower plate of the motor assembly. Try bending the head of the rivet upward to clear the plate. If that does not do the trick, then you need to replace the link assembly.

Holding-Tank Fix

I can't seem to find a kit for repairing a 1 × 1½-inch spot on a plastic freshwater tank. The tank appears to be very similar to those 1-gallon almost clear milk jugs, but only of a thicker gauge. Have I missed something?

HERBERT WODTKE
LOOGOOTEE, IL

Try the Syon Seal-N-Place Universal Plastic Tank Repair Kit available at most RV supply stores. This kit, which sells for around $14.95, uses an epoxy resin to repair holes up to 1 inch in diameter or cracks up to 5 inches in length. For larger jobs, you can combine any number of kits, although they are generally designed for making smaller repairs. The entire process takes approximately 20 minutes.

To make the repair, you first sand the surface, then mix the epoxy in the package and cut it open for application on the tank with the provided brush. The kit is complete, so you don't have to run to the hardware store for additional supplies.

Gray-Water Dilemma

My wife and I own a 1994 Prowler 275N fifth-wheel. Most of the time we stay at parks and campgrounds with full hookups, but occasionally we stay where there are limited facilities. We are usually quite content to stay for two or three days at these places because our freshwater and gray-water holding tanks are sufficient for this period of time. We can always find freshwater to refill that tank, but the gray-water tank is another matter.

Each of these tanks has a 40-gallon capacity. Would it be OK to install a pump and plumbing between the gray- and black-water tanks and transfer gray water to the black-water tank since this tank is never close to capacity after several days? This would extend our convenience for another day or two at places with no dump station. I realize that winterizing this system must also be done, but are there other considerations?

HAL ROSENQUIST
KING, NC

Hal, I suppose you could install a system to transfer gray water into the septic holding tank, but you need to be extremely careful not to allow black water to siphon back into the gray-water tank. Doing so would severely contaminate the tank and associated lines. Then you would have to live with the possibility of incredible stink throughout your RV.

Remember, the septic tank is relatively sealed from the rest of the plumbing in the rig and you should use chemicals to suppress smelly vapors that may escape when the toilet is flushed. If this "scent" is allowed to infiltrate the gray-water lines, you may never get the smell out of the coach. Every time you open a faucet, you'll be reminded.

If you insist on rigging up a line to pump waste water into the septic tank, use a very good quality check valve so that the flow cannot be reversed. Also, keep in mind that the flow of gray water from showering and/or doing the dishes can be rather fast. If it gets away from you—not paying attention to the monitor or an inaccurate monitor—you'll have a serious mess if the gray water causes the black-water tank to overfill and back up into the vent lines and/or the toilet when flushed.

I would use a portable gray-water tank to capture the overflow. That way you can empty it frequently while at camp and possibly extend your stay even longer. Make sure you use biodegradable soaps and be easy on the environment when dumping your portable tank. Many times you can dump the water in a primitive toilet at camp.

More on Waste

I have a Monomatic recirculating toilet that was made by Monogram Industries. I need parts for this toilet and I can't find the T-5 chemical treatment that it needs. Since I haven't been able to contact Monomatic, do you know where I can get parts? Is there another solution to replace the T-5? Can I make up a solution?

ANDY W. ADKINS
NEWPORT, RI

Andy, Monogram Sanitation is alive and well. You can reach them at 800 W. Artesia Blvd., Compton, CA 90224; (310) 638-8445. The company has plenty of parts available for your recirculating toilet. Monogram is very big in the public-sanitation business; you probably used one of its toilets if you visited a commercial jet's rest room.

The T-5 chemical is also in plentiful supply. Any RV dealer can order this product from its parts-distribution catalog. If your dealer can't (or won't), Monogram will be glad to accommodate your needs. It has a warehouse full of this stuff.

Holding Tank

After attending seminars on our sanitation system at Quartzite, AZ, Las Cruces, NM, and Phoenix last winter, we are confused. Some recommend using Rid X and Real Pine, while others said that these products will cause damage to the rubber seals. We began using the products after an RV seminar recommended them more than a year ago, but we are now wondering if continued use is going to cause damage to our system.

JAMES E. FINNMAN
HIGH RIVER, ALBERTA

According to Mary R. Burrows, who heads up Thetford Corp.'s staff of chemists, "Besides possibly causing damage to the sanitation system, there are safety considerations to keep in mind when mixing chemicals. When the wrong chemicals are mixed, they can cause violent reactions such as an explosion. Also, a combination of the wrong chemicals can result in a very toxic mixture."

Buying chemicals formulated specifically for RV use, such as those made by Thetford, will be properly labeled to eliminate the possibility of mishandling by the user. Of course, if the container is missing such instructions, referain from using the product.

Using household cleaners containing disinfectants or cleaners to which disinfectants have been added is also discouraged. Burrows says, "The reason for discouraging these products is because they are not formulated as deodorants, and many times are more detrimental to a waste-treatment system than the product designed and tested for this use."

Here are a few examples of how household items can damage expensive RV components: Petroleum-based products used to lubricate sticky valves can actually cause the seals to swell and crack (chemicals designed for holding tanks usually provide good lubrication for the seals). Pine cleaners may have good deodorizers but, since they are oil based, the seals can become damaged. Acids in most household toilet-bowl cleaners will also damage component seals. Keep in mind that the damage may progress slowly causing a failure at the most inopportune time.

What about the danger? It's hard to believe that using "simple" household chemicals can cause bodily harm, but it's true. For example, mixing household bleach with some holding-tank chemicals can cause an explosion. Therefore, if you don't know chemistry, refrain from brewing up household mixtures that may "seem" to do the job.

In a nutshell, it's better to be safe than sorry, even if it costs a little more money.

Bad Water

My question is one of concern, rather than technical. Is the water still OK to drink if it's been in the tank up to three months at 90- to 100-degree temperatures? We had our rig in storage so I felt like the water could become contaminated.

PHYLLIS SIELING
PALM COAST, FL

Allowing water to stand at any temperature is not wise, but in hot weather it's even worse. All kinds of things can grow in water when the temperature is high and there are no chemicals added to kill them. Yes, the water would be unsafe to drink.

The best advice is to empty your water tank at the end of every trip and refill before the next journey. If your tank has been contaminated, you should clean and disinfect it before using it again. To do this, first drain the tank and water heater completely. Then mix a ¼ cup of household bleach for every 15 gallons of tank capacity with 5 gallons of water. Pour this mixture into the tank and top off the tank with fresh water.

Drive around the block a couple of times to mix the solution. Run this water through all the spigots in the rig and the hot-water tank (remember this tank holds at least 6 gallons, so let the water run until it fills) and let the water stand for a couple of hours. Then drain the water system (including the hot-water tank). To remove any bad taste left by the bleach, repeat above procedure using ½ cup of baking soda mixed in a gallon of water poured into the water tank.

Detecting CO

I have a 1993 Flair motorhome with a CO*Star carbon-monoxide detector in it. The specifications supplied with the detector state that the battery life is one year. My battery has been lasting an average of about seven months. I wrote CO*Star to find out if there was a problem with my detector, or if the specifications have just been embellished considerably, but I have not received a response.

I have been looking at the 9-volt CO detector made by First Alert. The literature states a two-year limited warranty on the battery/sensor and that it will last up to three years. I have a First Alert smoke detector and the battery life is much longer than claimed, so I tend to believe the First Alert specifications. The First Alert CO detector at Home Depot is $35.90, compared to the CO*Star at Camping World for $84.50. The First Alert battery/sensor is $19.95 at Home Depot and is warranted to last two years. The battery and sensor for the CO*Star at Camping World is $11.50 and is supposed to last one year, but only lasts seven months. As you might guess, it has no warranty. The First Alert detector is warranted for six years. The CO*Star is warranted one year.

Will the First Alert be a satisfactory replacement for the CO*Star? At least I have confidence in the abilities and commitment of the First Alert products.

CHARLES WRIGHT
SAN DIEGO, CA

Charles, the CO*Star model 9A-i detector you have is hard on batteries. Although the specifications state that the battery life is one year, in real-world use it only lasts seven to eight months. According to Quantum Group Inc., the manufacturer of the CO*Star detector, the new model, 9B-i, has improved battery life of up to three years. The 9B-i has a single battery/sensor assembly that must be replaced as a package.

Fortunately, the CO*Star carbon-monoxide alarm will sound a beep about once every minute when the battery/sensor is weak. When this happens, the battery/sensor must be replaced immediately to continue protection. If you hold on to the 9A-i unit, make it a point to replace the battery and sensor every seven or eight months. It's a good practice to pick a date, write it down and follow a strict replacement schedule.

Although replacing batteries and sensors may seem like an expensive proposition, the cost involved is a mere pittance for the safety and peace of mind this device affords. As of September 1993, all motorized RVs and towables/campers equipped with auxiliary generators or fitted with AC generator-prep packages must be equipped with a carbon-monoxide detector.

In many cases these alarms may look like they are hard wired into the RV's electrical system, when in fact they are powered by a small internal battery. Make sure you understand how your CO detector functions and that it is maintained religiously. As long as the brand of CO detector you are considering is certified for use in RVs, it will meet code; most First Alert models are not.

Changing Carpet

We have a 1985 Winnebago with 45,000 miles that looks good as new inside and out, but my wife wants new carpet. When the unit was built, the carpet was laid and cabinets built over it. Can this carpet be cut at the bases of the cabinets and new carpet fitted and stapled down at the cabinets?

THERON S. BROWN
MORRESVILLE, NC

No problem, Theron, but you don't want to use staples. All you have to do is cut the carpet along the cabinets and walls, then add tack strips in all the areas where you made the cuts. Tack strips are thin, narrow pieces of wood that are nailed into the floor. As the carpet is stretched into position, the numerous tacks that protrude from the top are used to secure the carpet.

It's advisable to use a good carpet pad with this arrangement. You can rent a carpet stretcher from your local equipment rental yard or, if you prefer not to do it yourself, you can hire a professional carpet layer to do the job. In my experience, professionally laid carpet looks better and stays put over the long haul.

Shiny Cabinets

We have a 1977 Excel trailer and would like to know if there is a stain or varnish that we can use on the cabinets and walls. We have asked at paint stores, but haven't found anything to make them shine. Thank you for any help you can give us.

MR. AND MRS. KRAUS
ANAHEIM, CA

There are three types of wall and cabinet paneling used in RVs: photographic finish, vinyl covering and real wood. Extreme care must be taken when cleaning paneling with a photographic finish. Almost all cleaning materials will destroy this surface. Vinyl-coated paneling is more common in RVs. Great care must be exercised here, too. You are limited to using soap and water and you cannot scrub the surface, even though the panel is protected by a thin, clear vinyl.

Also, you should never use any adhesives, such as tape, or solvents, on these panels. To bring back the shine, try using 303 Protectant. This stuff works wonders on most finished surfaces. Real wood is much easier to care for. You should not have any problem cleaning these panels with a product formulated for this purpose; make sure you do not use abrasives. When it comes to replacing the original shine to the panel, try using Old English Furniture Polish. This stuff comes in both light and dark formulas and does a nice job. Of course, there are a number of fine products available at hardware and paint stores that will also restore the finish to your paneling.

Too Much Pressure

The crimped fittings on the ⅜-inch Qest plumbing in the hot-water system of my 1990 Gulfstream have begun failing like a row of dominoes. Each time I replace one with the gray compression-type fitting, the next crimped fitting lets loose. This is probably due to a freeze on the lot before I bought the unit.

Like all responsible RVers, I never connect to a freshwater supply without a 45-pound regulator. But in reading the manual for my Suburban water heater, I note that pressure in the hot-water system will reach 150 pounds during the heating cycle, limited by the pop-off valve, which I replaced just to make sure. What good is a 45-

pound regulator if half of the plumbing system is periodically subjected to 150 pounds of pressure, even for a short time?

BILL PYLE
OLYMPIA, WA

Good question, Bill. Your tank can build pressure up to 150 psi and that's why plumbing code provides for a relief valve that will "pop off" at this pressure. As long as there is air in the top of the tank, allowing a place for the expanding water (when heated) to go, the pressure in the lines will only increase slightly, well within the rating of the Qest lines.

The tank, though, can become water-logged whereby the air is dissolved into the water. If this happens, then it's possible for the pressure to build and work against the check valve in the city water fill and create problems for your water lines. To prevent this from happening, you need to drain your tank with the hot-water faucets open. Then close these faucets and turn the water pump on. Allow the tank to fill—until the water pump turns off—and light the water heater. When the water heater cycles off, slowly open each hot-water faucet until the water flows smoothly. This will provide the necessary air in the top of the tank.

If your pressure-relief valve starts weeping, I suspect you have a problem with the tank becoming partially water-logged. This is a good time to perform the above filling procedure. Better yet, do the above procedure at least once a year, preferably more often.

RV Antifreeze Facts

I'm a new member of the Good Sam Club, so I may ask a question that you have answered in the past. Is there any reason why windshield antifreeze (good down to −20°F) should not be used instead of more costly RV antifreeze to winterize the water system in my travel trailer? I even wonder if the two antifreeze solutions are the same except for the color?

DEMONT ROSEMAN JR.
CLEVELAND, NC

A few months ago we got a 1988 Jamee Class C motorhome from a man who had put automotive antifreeze in the freshwater tank and pumped it through the RV's system. Not aware it was the wrong type, I didn't check it until later—my mistake.

I can't find anyone with what I feel is correct and reliable information on the subject. Can you tell me what I need to do to the water system? The color of the antifreeze was light green. Prestone probably. Please advise.

KIOLEN CRIDER
KANNAPOLIS, NC

Both these people are flirting with death when it comes to winterizing the freshwater system in RVs. The antifreeze that is used in the windshield-washer fluid is most likely methanol or some alcohol derivative that is very toxic and, to put it mildly, can be dangerous to your health if ingested. Radiator antifreeze contains ethylene glycol, which is also poisonous to both animals and humans; death can occur if ingested. You should not use anything in your freshwater system except RV, nontoxic antifreeze designed for this purpose, period!

RV freshwater-system antifreeze is pink; the manufacturers purposely add color so that you will not be confused. Even though pink antifreeze is supposed to be nontoxic, it still makes sense to read the label before adding the solution to your water system. RV antifreeze uses a potable solution to prevent freezing that is nontoxic, but we still recommend that you refrain from drinking it. Make sure you flush the water system before drinking the water. If you are living in extreme cold conditions and find yourself adding RV antifreeze and purging the system daily to prevent freezing (and would rather not flush the system each day), you should drink bottled water until winter is over.

There are a couple of units on the market that make winterizing easier. Camco offers a Manual Winterizing System and a Push Button Winterizing kit that provides very convenient methods for distributing the antifreeze. Usually the process takes only a gallon or two of antifreeze. The electronic version uses solenoid valves to bypass the freshwater tank and water heater; the RV water pump is then used to draw antifreeze out of the kit's storage tank and distribute it throughout the water system. The electronic kit retails for around $486. For more information, Contact Camco Manufacturing Inc., 121 Landmark Drive, Greensboro, NC 27419; (919) 668-7661.

Potable antifreeze is more costly than the other types of mixtures on the market, but it sure beats the alternative while trying to save a few bucks.

Hubcaps

I have been told that installing hubcaps on the wheels of my Ford E-350 chassis contributes to overheating brakes because it reduces the amount of air that normally would be available for cooling. What do you think of that?

JACK H. KRAUSE
WILLOWICK, OH

I don't think you have much to worry about, Jack. The brakes get plenty of cooling from the back side. In any case, the wheel covers designed for motorhomes have large holes.

Camper Questions

We are thinking of buying a camper that we will be able to remove and have the truck available to drive at our destinations. What is the fastest and best way to take the camper on and off the truck? When the camper is off the truck it doesn't look good. Has anyone come up with a snap-on curtain that goes around the base of the camper or some other way to make it look better when off the truck? Is there a listing available that rates the trucks for campers or any articles that discuss the pros and cons of using a camper? I heard that windage and being top heavy can be a problem. Where is the best place to get a listing of all the campers available?

ROBERT CHAPMAN
PALATKA, FL

The most common way to load and unload a camper, Robert, is with the use of four-corner jacks. There are a number of systems on the market, the most popular being manual or electric screw-type jacks. Hydraulic jacks were the staple for many years, but lower-quality units on the market created potential safety problems. The good hydraulics, like those made by Happijac, work fine, but camper builders seem to gravitate toward screw-type jacks.

The electric jacks, of course, are easier and faster to use. Unloading is simply a matter of extending the corner jacks until the camper clears the truck. The truck is driven out from under the camper and the jacks retracted to a comfortable level. It's important to keep the camper properly balanced at all times while extending or retracting the jacks. If you don't have electric jacks, it's safer to use two people to operate each corner of the front or rear so the movement is uniform. It only takes about 20 minutes to remove or load the camper, once you get the hang of things.

If you plan on using a "stinger" to extend the hitch receiver on the truck (so you can tow one of your toys), then the job can become more difficult. Lining up the "stinger" into the bumper bracket can sometimes be very frustrating.

If you really want a slick way to load and unload your camper, consider a Jiffylift system by Happijac. As long as you have a camper floor that's at least 101 inches long, the Jiffylift system will work. The Jiffylift has been around for more than 25 years, but it seems to be ignored as a practical solution to loading and unloading. It uses a specially designed track that mounts to the underside of the camper and a removable cranking assembly that attaches to the truck; the hardware is relatively easy to install. It's only compatible with Happijac corner jacks (hydraulic or screw) because wheels must be attached to the feet of the rear jacks. In use, it only takes a few minutes to roll the camper off the truck and there is no unsightly hardware on the camper. Contact Happijac at 505 N. Kays Dr., Kaysville, UT 84037; (801) 544-2585.

I don't think anyone is making a universal camper curtain. I would contact a local canvas or upholstery shop and have one custom made.

As far as the pros and cons of camper ownership are concerned, I don't have room in this column for such a dissertation, but you can find all the camper manufacturers listed in the 1998 "RV Buyers Guide," published by *Trailer Life* and *MotorHome*. Call the Good Sam Club's Member Services Department at (800) 234-3450 to order a copy. You should have no adverse handling problems as long as the truck is rated to carry the weight of the camper.

Camper Stability

After much discussion with tire, camper and aftermarket vendors, I am still confused over the best approach to stabilize my slide-in camper during crosswind situations.

I have a 1992 Ford F-250 with camper/trailer package and 235/85R16 tires. We are hauling a 10-foot slide-in camper that weighs approximately 2,600 pounds. The truck/camper combination has been a pleasure to drive until a recent experience in a high crosswind caused me some concern.

What would you suggest as possible solutions to this potentially hazardous condition?

THOMAS H. MOSES JR.
WOODSIDE, CA

Tom, if your truck is rated properly for the camper and you have good tie-downs, there's little more you can do to improve stability. Keep in mind that extremely high crosswinds are tough on any high-profile vehicle, regardless of the equipment. Since you are happy with the stability during normal driving conditions, I suspect that your concern was based on the exceptionally high wind conditions during your recent experience. It's always best to sit out extremely high winds.

Make sure you are using a good-quality tie-down system. The best one on the market is made by the Happijac Co. It supplies camper anchors that mount to the bed and bumper of the truck and spring-loaded turnbuckles that attach the camper to the anchors. You also can try a rear anti-sway bar; your truck should be equipped with a front anti-sway bar. Also, make sure your shocks are in good working order.

Safety Glass

I have a 1991 29-foot Holiday Rambler Free Spirit travel trailer, purchased new from Holiday World Inc. in Houston. A recent storm produced hail stones that broke one of the side windows.

When I contacted a local glass company to fix it, the serviceman said it was window-pane glass and should be tempered glass. Another source also said the same thing. None of the windows have the safety-glass logo.

Where can I find out if there is a law that requires travel-trailer manufacturers to install tempered glass? Is it possible that this law applies only in certain states? The glass-company serviceman has told me they are going to replace the broken window with tempered glass since it is required. I need a third opinion from what I consider a very good source.

ALLEN G. BROWN
HOUSTON, TX

Safety glass is designed to reduce the possibility of flying pieces when broken (usually due to an impact) and is required by Federal Motor Vehicle Standard 205 for the windows in motorhomes, van conversions, campers and shells.

This federal standard is applicable to vehicles that are designed to carry passengers and is not required in travel trailers and fifth-wheels. There are, however, a handful of states that have their own laws on the use of safety glass in trailers and fifth-wheels.

The following states have safety-glass laws for both fifth-wheels and trailers: Connecticut, Delaware, New Jersey, North Carolina, Ohio, Tennessee, Virginia and Wisconsin. California requires its use for fifth-wheels only. As you can see, Texas has no safety-glass requirement. Therefore your dealer has no justification for refusing to install the same type glass that was originally provided in your trailer.

Water Spots on Glass

I have a 1987 Elite motorhome that has water spotting on the windshield and side glass. I have tried all the commercial cleaners and some of my own ideas like lemon, vinegar, mayonnaise and Goop (hand cleaner), but I am out of ideas. Other campers I've talked to are experiencing the same problem.

I haven't seen anything on this subject in *Highways* and I thought I would send in my question for publication to see if anyone out there has a solution.

BILL HAMM
WILDOMAR, CA

Bill, your letter really got me hot on the trail for products that would solve the water-spotting problem. I have the same problem with stubborn water spots and, until recently, could not find the remedy.

While snooping around a large automotive swap meet, I ran across a product called Pro Clean. The company markets a hard-water-spot mineral remover and sealant. I tried other products, including those "as seen on TV" and had not found one that really worked well until Pro Clean came along.

This stuff is not cheap, but having clear vision is worth the $25 I paid for one container of remover and one of sealant. The remover comes with a couple of scrubbing pads and very fine steel wool that can be used on real stubborn areas. The remover paste is rubbed into an area about the size of a baseball using a damp cloth. It's somewhat tedius, but the results are impressive. The sealer just wipes on and off and protects against future spotting.

Pro Clean is manufactured by Pacific Sun Makers, 2215 Grove Ave., Sacramento, CA 95815; (800) 921-6861 or (916) 921-6861. According to the manufacturer, the mineral-and-stain remover also is formulated to be used on tile, chrome, porcelain, aluminum, fiberglass and stainless steel.

Mice Be Gone!

In the June issue we tackled the problem of mice hanging out (and leaving evidence that they were) in RVs. Well, the reader response has been terrific. Many of the solutions are very creative. Some obviously work well and some really activated our funny bone. In any case, thanks for the letters.

The subject of mice was brought up and one of the responses was to spread Downy Fabric Softener (sheets) around the inside of the motorhome. We tried it by putting a full box, opened on one end, under the sink cabinet in the bathroom where the gray water goes into the holding tank. This was last summer. The box of Downy is still there and we have not seen any sign of mice.

BOB AND TOBY AHLMAN
CITCHFIELD, CT

We use some of the small "ultrasonic pest repellers" that you can purchase from mail-order houses. These plug into your electric outlets. They emit a high-frequency sound that you or your pets cannot hear but drives the mice crazy.

We've used these in a summer home and storage building and have not had a problem—with one exception. One came through the dryer vent and, after much evidence of trying to escape through the widows, it committed the ultimate and final sacrifice by jumping into the toilet.

CARROL E. HAMON
LONGMONT, CO

We have had RVs for approximately 20 years. We always used moth flakes until three or four years ago. We now buy camphor cakes at a drugstore. They are approximately $1 each if you buy a box of 12. Place these around the interior (closets, cupboards, in the sinks, etc.). These cakes come wrapped so I just prick a hole in the wrapper. They keep out all rodents and creepy crawlers plus have a "fresh" odor.

BILL PARRISH
CRANVILLE, VT

I stored my fifth-wheel under a big lean-to shed and, in no time at all, I think every field mouse in the country used it for a holiday resort. I beat the problem very easily. I bought a 100-foot roll of 24-inch hardware wire, the 1-inch hex-shaped wire cloth used in rabbit pens. I put it on 8-foot sections of framing and installed it like shirting around my fifth-wheel. Every night I put my two outside cats in the pen. I give them food and water, have a nice warm box for them to sleep in and a litter box. Every morning I let one section down so the cats are free to roam.

WES THORSEN
BROOKINGS, OR

I tried everything. These critters would eat through the engine wires and then some. I found Pest Away Ultra Shield professional protection. For more information, call (800) 950-2210. Beware: There are many cheap copies out there. Don't be fooled, this one really works.

FLOLRENCIO MARQUEZ
GLENDALE, CA

We were fishing on the Snake River and mice got into our motorhome. We caught several in traps and then put moth balls in each compartment. We put them in plastic containers and the mice ate the bottoms out. So we put the moth balls in tin containers—and no mice. Also, we put dog flea collars in the hot-water-tank and refrigerator compartments to keep spiders and ants out of there.

MR. AND MRS. LAWRENCE HENDRY
HERMISTON, OR

The solution is to go to a pet store and ask for used cage litter from either ferrets or from white rats (not white mice). Divide this up in small amounts and put it in nylon mesh bags—much as one would make small rice bags to throw after a wedding reception. Place these small bags in places in the RV where mice would normally enter. You don't need very many. The odor may be a little pungent for a while, but nothing compared to a dead mouse.

TERRY RIEGER
CASPER, WY

In reference to the mice problem, scatter mothballs in the unit to keep them away. We wrap the balls in pouches and put them in hidden areas when the unit is stored. Doing this makes it easy to gather them when using the unit.

JEAN SPECKMAN
ST. JAMES CITY, FL

Catch one mouse in a trap that will not harm it. Remove the mouse from the trap. Get a small can of red paint and an artist's brush. Paint the rear end of the mouse and let it dry. Then turn the mouse loose in the RV with the other mice. When the mice see the painted mouse, they will laugh themselves to death. Therefore, you have no use for traps, Comet, Decon or poison—and no cruelty.

C.C. McCOY
PASCAGOULA, MS

Best Place to Store

I am planning to join the snowbirds next winter in Yuma, Arizona. I have a 24-foot Airstream and will be in Las Vegas, Nevada in August. I want to store my trailer around there until I am ready to go to Yuma.

I understand that storing the trailer in hot weather is detrimental and can dry out the wood, among other effects. How would you recommend I store the trailer?

DAVE PERKINS
EAST WENATCHEE, WA

As a general rule, Dave, storing your trailer in drier climates is preferred. Warmer areas, where the humidity is low, helps keep rust and corrosion to a minimum and are not good breeding grounds for mildew. You'll be better off if you protect the trailer from direct sunlight, severe winds and blowing sand. Make sure the tires and all other rubber and vinyl surfaces are covered or treated monthly with a good protectant like 303. You should also keep a window and/or vent cracked for ventilation.

Some owners report that placing a small bucket filled with water in the RV is a good way to prevent the wood from cracking when stored in heat and low humidity. Of course, the bucket would have to be checked often. Also, keep in mind that storing your trailer for one season is not a problem, but RVs that are stored for long periods usually show signs of deterioration due to the elements.

If you are going to store the trailer in a muggy climate, you should keep a window and vent partially open so that air continues to circulate in an effort to remove condensation. Mildew and its associated odor are tough on fabrics and other materials and often hard to combat.

It's always best to seek shelter for all stored RVs and, if a formal structure is not available, then consider using a cover. But make sure the cover is designed for auto/RV use; these usually breathe and will protect against mildew and other surface damage due to intense heating and cooling.

CO Detector Worries

Our 1996 Bounder 28T is equipped with a factory-installed carbon-monoxide monitor. It is a Model SS933-CO-RV manufactured by Atwood Mobile Products.

Not long after taking delivery of our unit, we were rudely awakened in the wee hours by this CO monitor. At the time of the alarm, there was no possible source of CO to which the monitor could have responded. We were not using the furnace or any other gas-burning appliance. The frustration of the false alarm was amplified by our inability to deactivate or reset the alarm. Finally, by taping over the sensor openings, we were able to return to sleep.

Having no confidence in the reliability of the CO monitor, we have left it deactivated (sensor openings covered). Next, I wrote to Atwood and asked for advice. All this brought was another copy of the user's manual, devoid of any specific response. Have you had a similar experience with the CO monitor?

Another related comment: I was unable to locate a fuse that was labeled "CO monitor" or any equivalent notation. I realize that providing easy access to the power source is not advisable since this makes it simple to deactivate the monitor and leave it that way.

Short of pulling fuses one at a time, I have not pursued the search for the source of the minitor power. Any comments?

MILTON E. MCLAIN
LOS ALAMOS, NM

This is a sensitive issue, Milton. On one hand, it is a pain when the sensor goes off, waking you in the middle of the night. But on the other hand, the results could have been disastrous if the alarm was real. Remember, carbon monoxide is odorless and colorless and can kill the occupants in a very short time. What's more, CO detectors are required in all RVs equipped with an AC generator or factory prepared to accept an auxiliary power plant.

Many times the alarm can be set off by the fumes released from the paneling, carpeting and upholstery in a new RV. This usually happens on hot days when the rig is not adequately ventilated. The manufacturers of CO detectors will even till you that these devices need to "settle into the environment" before they quit sounding false alarms.

The CO detector has a component-failure feature built into the circuit. If the detector has failed, a solid orange light will illuminate and the audible section will chirp every 90 seconds, or a solid red light will come on and a continuous alarm will be somewhat muffled. If this happens, you need to send the unit back to the company for service or replacement.

If the detector monitor shows no failure during the sounding of the alarm, then you should always suspect that it is working properly and take action to ventilate the interior with fresh air. Even though you did not have the furnace or AC generator operating at the time, any number of circumstances could have set off the alarm. For instance, a neighboring RV with the AC generator running and the wind blowing just right could have allowed exhaust gases to enter your coach. An engine idling close by can do the same.

The detector you have has a number of built-in lights and alarms to notify the user of operational problems. I would use these to diagnose any problems and return the detector to the manufacturer if you determine that it is not working properly.

Your detector should have been wired at the factory in a fail-safe manner. Some models even have backup connections to another source of power in case of a battery failure. Forget about finding the wire to deactivate the alarm and restrain yourself from taping over the sensor holes. CO detectors are important; making sure they work right will bring peace of mind and safety to your RV adventures.

Beat the Dust

We will be leaving soon on a trip to Alaska in a Class C motorhome. While reviewing *Canada's Yukon, The Official Vacation Guide*, the following appeared in an article about Yukon highway driving: "To control dust in your camper or trailer, reverse the roof vent on your rig so that the vent hatch faces forward. While driving keep the hatch open a few inches, creating inside air pressure to control the dust."

Since the roof vents, when opened, always face rearward, wouldn't it be a better approach to keep them tightly closed while driving?

JIM KUCABA
ORANGE, CA

Jim, anytime you can pressurize the interior of a vehicle, you limit the intrusion of dust. That's why it makes sense to close the windows and run the heater fan when driving a vehicle on a very dusty road. The same is true when turning the vent around. By leaving a small opening, the air being forced in pressurizes the interior. This will help prevent dust from getting through small openings. Remember, no trailer is absolutely airtight.

The key here is to only open the vent slightly. If you open it too far, the wind will rip the lid from its mounting hardware. When the vent is open in a conventional manner, a venturi effect can allow the trailer interior to suck dust in from the small openings. Make sure you close the lid—or set it up in reverse for dusty roads—when you break camp.

Rotten Floor

I noticed a spot under the couch in my 31-foot trailer where the water hose connects on the outside. I found no leak when I checked the water line. Further checking gave me a big surprise: The floor was rotted out all around the perimeter of the trailer anywhere from 3 to 12 inches wide. I am wondering if condensation has created this problem?

If I went to buy another trailer just like this one, how can I tell if it is rotted out by the way the trailer is built? I had to cut the underbelly material and wade through the Styrofoam insulation to find the condition of the floor. It was very wet and full of tiny ants and mold. The wood just falls out. Please help.

CECIL A. CHRISTMAN
IRVINGTON, AL

I don't believe the problem is condensation, Cecil. More likely, there's a leak somewhere—or a number of leaks. First, pressure-check the water system. This can be easily done by running the water pump until it cycles off. If it continues to blip, suspect a leak; if it remains quiet, then there's no leak and you can confirm your observation that the water lines are probably secure. Check the water tank. It's possible that a fitting for the hose to the inlet of the pump is leaking or there's a crack somewhere, but this may not be the problem if the trailer has always been stored with the tank empty.

Unfortunately, there are many places for water to leak into the trailer. When the perimeter of the rig is wet, I always start with the window frames. Make sure they are sealed properly with butyl tape and that the weep holes in the bottom of the frame are not plugged. Next, check the clearance lights. These puppies can cause more problems than you can imagine. Make sure the vents on the roof are sealed properly and that the air-conditioner seal is good. And, of course, make sure the roof seams—if any—are sealed. Check that the roof-lap seams around the edges of the trailer are secure and sealed properly. Although the roof may seem like "miles away" from the floor perimeter, remember that water can travel anywhere it's not restricted. Usually you'll find signs of roof leakage inside the overhead compartments and in the corners of the ceiling.

Water leakage usually leaves a good trail. You should be able to follow the rotted wood to the source of the leak(s). If you inspect your next trailer carefully—and perform regular checks—your confidence should return.

Index